PowerPC

AN INSIDE VIEW

Michael Koerner, Chak Ming Fai and Joe Ruthven

D1609416

PRENTICE HALL PTR, UPPER SADDLE RIVER, NEW JERSEY 07458

For information about redbooks:
http://www.redbooks.ibm.com/redbooks

Send comments to:
redbooks@vnet.ibm.com

Published by

Prentice Hall PTR
Prentice-Hall, Inc.
A Simon & Schuster Company
Upper Saddle River, NJ 07458

The publisher offers discounts on this book when ordered in bulk quantities. For more information, contact

Corporate Sales Department,
Prentice Hall PTR
One Lake Street
Upper Saddle River, NJ 07458
Phone: 800-382-3419; FAX: 201-236-714
E-mail (Internet): corpsales@prenhall.com

For book and bookstore information

http://www.prenhall.com

Printed in the United States of America

10 9 8 7 6 5 4 3 2 1

ISBN 0-13-255753-3

Prentice-Hall International (UK) Limited, *London*
Prentice-Hall of Australia Pty. Limited, *Sydney*
Prentice-Hall Canada Inc., *Toronto*
Prentice-Hall Hispanoamericana, S.A., *Mexico*
Prentice-Hall of India Private Limited, *New Delhi*
Prentice-Hall of Japan, Inc., *Tokyo*
Simon & Schuster Asia Pte. Ltd., *Singapore*
Editora Prentice-Hall do Brasil, Ltda., *Rio de Janeiro*

Contents

Figures

Tables

Preface

This document provides technical details on the PowerPC technology. It focuses on the features and advantages of the PowerPC Architecture and includes an historical overview of the development of the reduced instruction set computer (RISC) technology.

It also provides technical details about the capability of IBM Personal Computer Power Series and the IBM ThinkPad Power Series.

It describes in detail the IBM Power Series product family based on PowerPC technology, including IBM Personal Computer Power Series 830 and 850 and IBM ThinkPad Power Series 820 and 850. Some knowledge of general PC technology is assumed.

How This Document Is Organized

The document is organized as follows:

- Chapter 1, "PowerPC Concepts"

  The introduction gives an overview of the personal computer market today, explains the market needs for PowerPC technology and defines the term "architecture." Furthermore, it provides information on the reduced instruction set computer (RISC) history, and the PowerPC alliance.

- Chapter 2, "Inside the PowerPC Technology"

  This chapter describes the different levels of the PowerPC Architecture and provides details on the PowerPC technology.

- Chapter 3, "RISC versus CISC"

  This provides details on the technology differences between the RISC and complex instruction set computer (CISC) technology as well as a road map on available CISC and PowerPC processors and performance details.

- Chapter 4, "PowerPC Strategy"

  This chapter provides insights into the PowerPC Reference Platform specification and the PowerPC Microprocessor Hardware Reference Platform.

- Chapter 5, "PowerPC Software Environment"

  This chapter discusses the PowerPC software environment including the different PowerPC operating systems, PowerPC application support and PowerPC application development tools.

- Chapter 6, "PowerPC - Hardware and Product Overview"

This provides detailed technical information on the IBM Power Series product line, including the IBM Personal Computer Power Series and the IBM ThinkPad Power Series.

- Appendix A, "What Is Multiprocessing?"

  This appendix is provided as an overview for readers who are not familiar with multiprocessing concepts.

- Appendix B, "The PowerPC Instruction Set"

  This appendix provides a list of the PowerPC Architecture instruction set.

Related Publications

The publications listed in this section are considered particularly suitable for a more detailed discussion of the topics covered in this document:

- *Inside the PowerPC Revolution*, ISBN 1-883577-04-7

- *PowerPC Computing*, ISBN 1-56529-625-7

- *PowerPC A Practical Companion*, ISBN 0-7506-1801-9

- *Computer Organization and Architecture*, ISBN 0-02-946297-5

- *PowerPC Processor Architecture*, 52G7487

- *PowerPC 601 Microprocessor User's Manual*, 52G7484

- *PowerPC System Technical Manual*, 52G7490

- *PowerPC AIX Hardware Dependencies Reference Guide*, 52G7485

- *IBM RISC System/6000 Technology*, IBM SA23-2619-00

A complete list of International Technical Support Organization publications, with a brief description of each, may be found in *International Technical Support Organization Bibliography of Redbooks, GG24-3070*.

Special Notices

This publication is intended to help IBM customers, dealers, system engineers and consultants to get a clear understanding on the capabilities of the IBM Power Series product line. The information in this publication is not intended as the specification of any programming interfaces that are provided by OS/2, AIX or any other operating system mentioned in this publication. See the PUBLICATIONS section of the IBM Programming Announcement for more information about what publications are considered to be product documentation.

References in this publication to IBM products, programs or services do not imply that IBM intends to make these available in all countries in which IBM operates. Any reference to an IBM product, program, or service is not intended to state or imply that only IBM's product, program, or service may be used. Any functionally equivalent program that does not infringe any of IBM's intellectual property rights may be used instead of the IBM product, program or service.

Information in this book was developed in conjunction with use of the equipment specified, and is limited in application to those specific hardware and software products and levels.

IBM may have patents or pending patent applications covering subject matter in this document. The furnishing of this document does not give you any license to these patents. You can send license inquiries, in writing, to the IBM Director of Licensing, IBM Corporation, 500 Columbus Avenue, Thornwood, NY 10594 USA.

The information contained in this document has not been submitted to any formal IBM test and is distributed AS IS. The information about non-IBM (VENDOR) products in this manual has been supplied by the vendor and IBM assumes no responsibility for its accuracy or completeness. The use of this information or the implementation of any of these techniques is a customer responsibility and depends on the customer's ability to evaluate and integrate them into the customer's operational environment. While each item may have been reviewed by IBM for accuracy in a specific situation, there is no guarantee that the same or similar results will be obtained elsewhere. Customers attempting to adapt these techniques to their own environments do so at their own risk.

Any performance data contained in this document was determined in a controlled environment, and therefore, the results that may be obtained in other operating environments may vary significantly. Users of this document should verify the applicable data for their specific environment.

The following document contains examples of data and reports used in daily business operations. To illustrate them as completely as possible, the examples contain the names of individuals, companies, brands, and products. All of these names are fictitious and any similarity to the names and addresses used by an actual business enterprise is entirely coincidental.

Reference to PTF numbers that have not been released through the normal distribution process does not imply general availability. The purpose of including these reference numbers is to alert IBM customers to specific information relative to the implementation of the PTF when it becomes available to each customer according to the normal IBM PTF distribution process.

You can reproduce a page in this document as a transparency, if that page has the copyright notice on it. The copyright notice must appear on each page being reproduced.

The following terms are trademarks of the International Business Machines Corporation in the United States and/or other countries:

AIX	AT
C Set ++	CICS
CT	DB2/2
IBM	IMS
Micro Channel	Operating System/2
OS/2	PAL
Personal System/2	PowerPC
Power Series 830	Power Series 820
Power Series	Power Series 850
PowerPC 601	PowerPC 603
PowerOpen	PowerPC Architecture
PowerPC Reference Platform	POWER Architecture
PowerPC 604	POWER Team
PowerPC 603e	Presentation Manager
PS/ValuePoint	PS/1
PS/2	RISC System/6000
RS/6000	System/360
System/370	ThinkPad
TrackPoint	VoiceType
400	

The following terms are trademarks of other companies:

A/UX, Apple, Apple Desktop Bus, Finder, GeoPort, LocalTalk, Mac,
  Macintosh, and System 7 are trademarks of Apple Computer, Incorporated
Alliance is a trademark of American Telephone and Telegraph Company
ATM is a trademark of Adobe Systems Incorporated
C++ is a trademark of American Telephone and Telegraph Company, Incorporated
Canon is a trademark of Canon Kabushiki Kaisha
C-bus is a trademark of Corollary, Inc.
Centronics is a trademark of Centronics Data Computer Corporation

Chapter 1. PowerPC Concepts

When we look at the history of computers and, specifically, the personal computer market, it is not difficult to observe the change. In its short life span, the PC business has advanced exponentially. As prices have decreased, performance has continuously increased and advanced.

The microprocessor design has played a very important role in this technological boom. Ironically, the architecture that controlled all the hardware and software design was defined long ago. This architecture was designed for the technology of its time but it still drives most of our personal computers today. It is for this reason that the term "backward-compatible" has become part of our day-to-day vocabulary.

For the last decade there has been only one predominant choice of processor in the personal computer world: the complex instruction set computer (CISC) technology on which microprocessor design was based. The market is totally based on the Intel and Motorola technology, which are not even compatible with each other.

Microprocessor technology was invented in 1970 by Ted Hoff, a young Intel engineer. His work was done for a Japanese company called Busicom, which was in the hand-held calculator business. Intel itself thought at the time that this processor was too limited to be useful.

The breakthrough came when BASIC began to be widely used. BASIC, a simple programming language, demonstrated that such a microprocessor could act very well as the central processing unit (CPU) in a computer system. The real business breakthrough came with Visicalc, the first spreadsheet application.

Today more than 165 million PCs have been sold, based on Intel and Motorola microprocessors. New applications and technologies, such as 3-D graphics and multimedia, require more and more CPU power, and CISC processors are struggling to provide this.

Today we have:

- Computation (spreadsheets, CAD)
- 2-D graphics
- Video and audio

Tomorrow we will have:

- Even more computation
- 3-D graphics
- Voice and language services
- Collaborative computing

Users today are expecting PCs to improve their productivity, but what we see is:

- Proliferation of devices with unique functions
- Multiple communication paths
- Restrictive human/system interface

Although today's personal computers are still driven by an architecture of the 70s, it is not because the field of computer architecture has not kept pace with technology. John Cocke from the IBM T. J. Watson Research Center started investigations in the mid-70s on approaches to improve processor performance. He found out that 80 percent of code was only using 20 percent of the available instructions in the processor. Eighty percent of the available instructions were either never used or could be replaced by using instruction strings of the 20 percent normally used.

As a result of this research and other projects of the time, a new approach to microprocessor design called reduced instruction set computer (RISC) evolved in the early 1980s.

A resounding testimonial to the importance of RISC is that all new processor designs over the last five years have been based on RISC technology.

The question today is no longer if personal computers will move to RISC technology, but when.

1.1 What Is an Architecture and Why Do We Need It?

Computer architecture refers to those attributes of a system that are visible to a programmer, or those attributes that have a direct impact on the logical execution of a program.

Historically, computer manufacturers have offered a family of computer models. These models all have had the same architecture although they may have had different components, price/performance values, etc. Architectures typically have survived many years while everything else around them has changed constantly.

One of the most successful systems on the market was the System/360 developed by IBM in the 60s. Revolutionary technology was to use integrated circuits (ICs); the instruction set was directly installed in the processor in the form of microcode.

Software compatibility across all System/360 models was the big advantage, since all System/360s had common instructions.

The System/360 was replaced by the IBM System/370 architecture. This architecture was first introduced in 1971 and included a number of models. IBM introduced many models over the years with improved technology offering the customer greater speed, lower cost or both. These newer models retained the same architecture as the other 370s so the customer's software investment was protected.

The term architecture is used to refer to a broad assortment of things in the computer industry. In the context of microprocessor architecture, it refers to the specifications upon which the design of a processor or family of processors is based. The architecture consists of the instruction set, the programming model, the exception model and other specifications that characterize a set of compatible processors. The need for a new architecture arises from the fact that the microprocessors in most of today's personal computers suffer from bottlenecks that are caused from outgrowing their original design.

In order to prevent the same situation that has happened with the original IBM Personal Computer, IBM has drawn up a document known as the PowerPC Reference Platform specification. This document gives guidelines and requirements for producing personal computer using PowerPC processors. Apple, IBM and Motorola have joined focus to produce the PowerPC Microprocessor Hardware Reference Platform. This architecture combines the Power Macintosh and PowerPC Reference Platform features. These documents are available free from IBM. For information on obtaining a copy of the PowerPC Reference Platform specification, refer to 4.1, "PowerPC Reference Platform Specification" on page 4-1.

1.2 The RISC Story

Contrary to popular belief, RISC architecture was born from an IBM project intended to solve a very specific problem. It was not created in an attempt to solve the fundamental problems of general purpose computing. Nor was it developed to provide a common architecture for a wide spectrum of processor requirements.

What really happened was that in 1974, IBM engineers needed a system to manage a telephone switching network. The network had to be capable of executing more than 20,000 instructions per call and 300 calls per second. No computer available at the time complied with this sort of real-time design criteria.

The absence of such a computer could cause arithmetic functions to quickly pile up, waiting to get access to the memory bus. This resulted in the memory bus becoming a tremendous bottleneck.

In order to meet the project specification, IBM engineers and designers envisioned a machine with simple instructions and extensive and well-placed on-chip memory. The latter are two fundamental characteristics of RISC technology today.

Reduced instruction set computing (RISC) consists of instructions that reduce operations into simpler tasks. These simple instructions each take approximately the same time to execute. In other words, reduce the instruction set and use a fixed length for the instruction so that in each clock cycle one instruction per computational unit can be executed. This makes it easier for the processor to interpret instructions, and it speeds up the execution while greatly simplifying processor design. Furthermore, once you have simple instructions, the compiler can optimize more easily the code to utilize the processor fully.

Although the telephone switching system was never built, the processor designers went on to explore further the possibilities presented by the project. The idea also created excitement in academic circles, and by the middle 70s there were several design projects underway:

- IBM 801 minicomputer

  Further development of the telephone switching principle led to the design of the 801. The 801 was developed by John Cocke in the mid-1970s.

- RISC-I and RISC-II

  David Patterson and his colleagues at the University of California developed the RISC-I and RISC-II processors and coined the term RISC.

- Stanford MIPS

  This machine was developed by John Hennessy and colleagues at the Stanford University.

These three projects exploited the principle of IBM's telephone switching design by taking advantage of simple, fixed-length instructions. RISC offered an exciting alternative to the prevailing philosophy of complex instruction set computing (CISC) processor design.

The success of these projects sparked considerable interest on the part of major established computer manufacturers. The university projects brought RISC design principles out of the laboratories and into the research and development efforts of commercial chip manufacturers.

Today many types of RISC implementations exist. RISC design, however, is most closely associated with a handful of microprocessor manufacturers whose products are intended mostly for use in high-end workstations. RISC design is still maturing and taking hold in more and more environments. RISC designers are constantly capitalizing on other technological advances, and as manufacturing processes improve, so do the chips. Transistor miniaturization has made it possible to have more and more transistors per square millimeter. The combination of cheaper circuits and simpler instructions has moved RISC processors from multi-chip designs to single-chip processors with caches, parallel floating point units (FPUs) and main memory units (MMUs).

These designs have resulted in the availability of RISC processors on the desktop. With the development of the PowerPC 603 power-saving processor, even low-power battery-operated notebook systems and palm-top computers are now available with RISC technology.

1.3 The PowerPC Alliance

History has proven that being the technology leader does not guarantee a successful product. Probably the best example of this is Beta and VHS video recording technology. Beta, clearly the better technology, has lost out to the strength of marketing and alliance of VHS.

The computer industry has seen its own fair share of alliance and marketing effects. The best example is definitely Microsoft Windows 3.1. Although it is seen by few people as a technology leader, it has become a de facto standard for personal computers. This snowballing effect of its popularity was achieved with the marketing strength of Microsoft and the alliances it formed to promote Windows as the default operating system.

Customers are not buying machines anymore for performance only. It is also important to look at the long-term viability of the chosen architecture. The viability of the architecture as a long-term solution relies on the acceptance of the direction of the technology and the ability of the alliance partners to promote these ideas in the market.

It is for this reason that the success of the PowerPC-based systems rests as much on market acceptance, openness and direction of the industry and alliances supporting the PowerPC initiatives as it does on the exciting advances embodied in the PowerPC family of processors and, more specifically, the IBM Power Series.

We will now briefly look at the alliance, its goals and objectives.

1.3.1 PowerPC Alliance, Goals and Objectives

The Somerset Design Center in Austin, Texas was created as a result of the alliance formed between IBM, Apple and Motorola in October 1991. It was on this date that the three companies announced they would jointly develop a new architecture that would form the basis of the next generation of personal computers.

The alliance recognized that the computer industry is one of the most rapidly growing industries in the world and that more and more computer power is required to fulfill customer application requirements.

The alliance set for itself the following objectives:

- Object-oriented technology
- Interconnectivity and networking
- Open system environment
- Microprocessor technology
    - Permit broad range of implementations
    - Simplify to reduce design cycle time
    - Allow for aggressive superscalar implementations
    - Support symmetrical multiprocessors (SMP)
    - Define a 64-bit superset architecture which provides binary compatibility for 32-bit POWER applications

The objectives were achieved when the first PowerPC microprocessor, the PowerPC 601, was announced to the industry in 1992 and began shipment in early 1993.

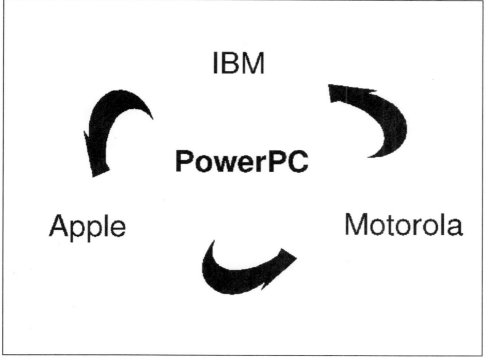

Figure   1-1. *The PowerPC Alliance*

The PowerPC alliance provides greater opportunities for compatibility and more efficient mixed network environments. One product of this collaboration is an IBM-certified Apple token-ring card. It also inspired the following joint efforts:

- Kaleida Labs

  Kaleida is a new company funded by IBM and Apple to create common standards for the fast-growing multimedia products.

- Taligent

  Taligent is also a new company funded by IBM and Apple that is developing an object-oriented operating system.

- PowerOpen

  PowerOpen is aimed towards developing a new version of the UNIX operating system that will combine features from IBM's AIX and Apple's A/UX operating systems. This platform will allow users access to AIX and Macintosh-based applications.

1.3.2 The History of the PowerPC Alliance

The following section will give chronological descriptions of the events surrounding and following the announcement of the PowerPC alliance.

In October 1991, IBM, Apple and Motorola jointly announced the formation of a new alliance. At that time, details were presented for the first time about the PowerPC Architecture and the PowerOpen environments.

Bull HN Information Systems, Inc., announced adoption of the new PowerPC Architecture for their server and workstation systems in January 1992.

During April 1992, Thomsonn-CSF CEITIA announced an agreement with IBM to develop products based on the PowerPC Architecture.

In May 1992, IBM, Apple and Motorola dedicated the Somerset Design Center in Austin, Texas.

The first processor was manufactured and unveiled by IBM, Apple and Motorola in October 1992. The chip was called the PowerPC 601.

The Harris corporation announced an agreement with IBM to develop real-time workstations based on the PowerPC Architecture in November 1992.

In December 1992 Tadpole Technology PLC announced an agreement with IBM to develop and produce notebook computers based on the PowerPC Architecture.

Thomson-CSF CETIA announced PowerPC VME systems and Lynx real-time software in January 1993.

In March 1993, Apple, Bull, Harris, Motorola, Tadpole Technology and Thomson-CSF announced the formal founding of the PowerOpen Association with the goal of providing an open system and compatibility.

During April of 1993 SunSoft announced plans to support Solaris on PowerPC based systems. In the same month Motorola announced general sampling of the PowerPC 601.

IBM and Motorola announced the availability of the PowerPC 601 tools catalog in May 1993, together with an announcement from Ford that the next generation of their Power Train Electronic Controller would be based on PowerPC Architecture.

Kaleida Labs, Scientific Atlanta and Motorola announced plans for interactive multimedia devices, developed using PowerPC processors in June 1993.

October 1993 was quite a busy month for the PowerPC alliance. An 80MHz version of the 601 was announced and the PowerPC 603 reached first silicon. CETIA, a subsidiary of Thomson-CSF, introduced a family of VME single-board computers and workstation based on the PowerPC 601 processor.

Bull also announced their first PowerPC-based system. Three systems configurations were made available: a compact desktop server, a desk side server and a single-user workstation. These systems are based on the PowerPC 601 processor.

Motorola's RISC Microprocessor division also announced in October five software development packages for optimizing performance of the PowerPC 603.

In the same month Apple announced the commitment from seven additional software developers. These developers also announced plans to ship upgraded versions of the software simultaneously with the first PowerPC systems.

IBM announced the PowerPC Personal System in November 1993. The PowerPC Reference Platform specification is a non-proprietary standard developed by the IBM Power Personal Systems Division, with participation from others in the industry. Operating systems planned to be ported to the PowerPC Reference Platform specification include AIX, OS/2, Windows NT, Solaris, and Taligent.

Also, in November 1993, Microsoft and Motorola announced that a port of Windows NT was jointly being developed with IBM's Power Personal Systems Division. The port to Windows NT, which conforms to the PowerPC Reference Platform specification, operates in Little-Endian mode and takes advantage of the PowerPC's Bi-Endian feature. A broad group of computer subsystem manufacturers announced support for the PowerPC Reference Platform specification.

In February 1994 Insignia Solutions and Apple announced an agreement to include SoftWindows in selected configurations of PowerPC-based Macintosh systems.

In November 1994, Apple, IBM and Motorola announced the PowerPC Microprocessor Hardware Reference Platform. This platform will combine features of the Power Macintosh and PowerPC Reference Platform specification.

Chapter 2. Inside the PowerPC Technology

The PowerPC processor is a third-generation RISC architecture which has evolved from IBM's POWER (Performance Optimization With Enhanced RISC) architecture. Many features and design points of the POWER Architecture, such as superscalar design, zero-cycle branching and a highly optimized cache structure, have been retained in the PowerPC Architecture. These concepts will be explained in the next section, which starts the discussion of the PowerPC Architecture with a look at the POWER Architecture. Although the motivating factors that drive the design of the PowerPC Architecture differ from those for the POWER Architecture in many aspects, the decisions that were made in the design of the POWER architecture remain the same for the PowerPC processors. In order to understand the PowerPC, we first have to understand its heritage.

Next, we will discuss some general concepts of computer architecture that help us to understand the various features of the PowerPC Architecture.

Section 2.3, "The PowerPC Architecture" on page 2-23 and 2.4, "Elements of the PowerPC Architecture" on page 2-28 will examine the PowerPC Architecture in general and the elements defined by it.

We will conclude with a look at some current and planned implementations of PowerPC processors.

2.1 The POWER Architecture and the RISC System/6000

IBM introduced the RISC System/6000 family of products to the market in 1990. The goal then was to offer a series of products that would satisfy customer requirements for commercial and scientific applications. The first RS/6000 products were implementations of the POWER Architecture. The POWER Architecture is a second-generation RISC Architecture which contained many innovations for its time as well as major advances over existing RISC architectures. These innovations and advances were necessary to meet some design goals. These goals were motivated by various driving factors.

2.1.1 The Driving Factors

The POWER Architecture was designed to address the requirements of a UNIX-based system family and could effectively support both commercial application and scientific environments. This key objective arose out of several driving factors which occurred mainly in the late 1970s and early 1980s:

- A growing market of commercial, engineering and scientific applications running on UNIX-based systems. In order to participate and lead in this growing market segment, IBM had to develop a very robust and flexible architecture on which good products could be built.

- Emergence of RISC designs and implementations from various manufactures.

- Availability of 1 micron CMOS VLSI circuit technology that allowed 300,000 to one million devices per chip and projected clock cycles of 25 to 30MHz. Clearly, this technology advance could be exploited to develop a more powerful architecture.

- New developments in the fields of compiler technology and computer organization and architecture, both within and outside of IBM. Again, there was an opportunity to exploit these new discoveries to bring to market more advanced products.

2.1.2 POWER - The Design Goals

The key objective of the RS/6000 family of products was to be able to support both commercial and scientific application environments effectively. This implied that the underlying processor architecture had to efficiently fulfill the unique requirements of processing in both environments. In particular:

- Commercial environments generally feature more integer processing, transaction processing and file I/O. Therefore, the key components that would influence performance are the integer processing component of the CPU and the I/O subsystem.

- Scientific and engineering environments usually require very high floating-point computation performance. To be able to support these environments effectively, the architecture must have a scheme to optimize floating-point performance.

An important goal of any processor architecture design is to minimize execution time. In the design effort of the POWER Architecture, this was viewed as the product of three important factors: path length, cycles per instruction, and cycle time.

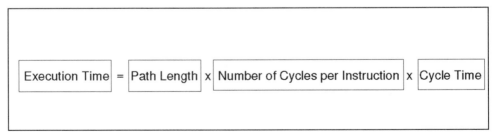

Figure **2-1.** *The Definition of Execution Time*

- *Execution Time* is defined as *Path Length* times *Cycles per Instruction* times *Cycle Time*. An improvement in any of the three variables can result in a corresponding improvement in execution time.

- *Path Length* can be roughly defined as the number of instructions which are needed to perform a certain piece of work. This variable is largely influenced by the instruction set architecture and how well optimizing compilers do their job.

- *Cycles per Instruction* can be viewed as the throughput of the CPU. It is the average number of clock cycles needed to complete executing one instruction. Generally, the factors influencing throughput are the processor architecture and the compiler technology.

- *Cycle Time* is the clock speed of the processor (the MHz). It is a measure of how much time the processor takes to complete one clock cycle. Much of this depends on the chip technology and the processor architecture.

It is important to note that in the equation above, the three variables are not independent of each other. There are interactions between the factors that influence more than one of the three variables. For example, if the instruction set and processor architecture is very simple, it is probably easier to make the CPU run at a faster clock speed (reduced cycle time). But with a simple instruction set, more instructions would be needed to perform a piece of work compared to an architecture with a more complex instruction set (longer path length). These interdependences complicated the work of designing the architecture. Thus, a decision was made to focus the design work on *reduced instruction set cycles*, which was defined as the optimal value of *Path Length* times *Cycles per Instruction*. In this way, RISC was basically redefined to have the objective of reducing the execution time through reducing the *instruction set cycles* instead of simply reducing the *instruction set*.

2.1.3 Inside the POWER Architecture

The result of the design process to meet the goals stated above was the POWER Architecture, a highly concurrent, superscalar enhancement of early RISC architectures.

The POWER Architecture has many similar features to earlier, more traditional RISC architectures:

- Register-oriented instruction set

- Simple, fixed-length instructions

- A hardwired, as opposed to microcoded, CPU

- Strong pipelining features

These concepts will be explained in Chapter 3, "RISC versus CISC" on page 3-1.

Where POWER differs from first-generation RISC architectures is its use of advanced features, such as:

- Multiple instruction dispatch
- Multiple execution units, permitting simultaneous execution of different types of instructions
- Separate instruction and data caches
- Zero-cycle branches

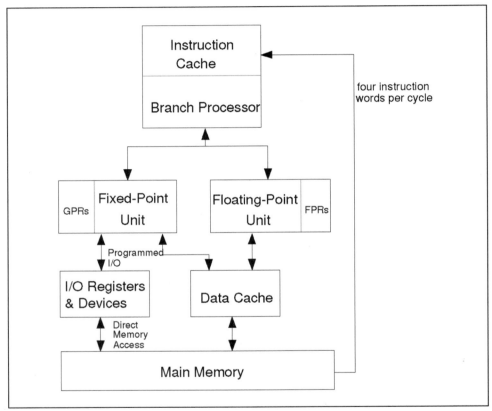

Figure *2-2. Block Diagram of the POWER Architecture*

Figure 2-2 shows a logical view of the basic POWER architecture. There are three main execution units in the CPU:

- The *fixed-point unit* (FXU) performs operations on whole numbers without a decimal point (for example, numbers like 3, 6 and 24) and numeric representations of text. It contains the general-purpose registers (GPRs) and the arithmetic logic unit, which does the actual execution. The FXU also carries out the duty of address translation. Address translation is the process of calculating the actual address in real memory of a piece of data from the virtual addresses which are used in programs to point to data. This process is necessary when the CPU needs to access data from main memory.

- The *floating-point unit* (FPU) performs mathematical operations on numbers with a decimal point. These kinds of numbers are common in scientific and engineering applications. Unlike typical floating-point coprocessors, the FPU in the POWER Architecture is closely coupled to the rest of the CPU and can execute instructions independently of the other execution units. A unique feature of the POWER Architecture is that it implements the multiply-add floating-point instruction (an operation of the form AxB+C). This instruction is executed with the same delay as a single multiply or add instruction and is, effectively, two instructions in one.

- The *branch processor* is implemented within the instruction cache unit (ICU). It independently executes all branch and condition register instructions. Branch instructions are instructions that cause the flow of the execution to be redirected to some other part of the program. Condition register operations are instructions that operate on information about the results of earlier calculations (for example, is A=B or X>Y?).

The basic POWER Architecture has a highly optimized cache structure which specifies separate instruction and data caches. Cache memory is very high-speed storage that buffers data and instructions between the slower main memory system and higher-speed CPU registers.

The instruction cache unit (ICU) reads four instructions at a time from main memory. This bandwidth is very important, as we will see later. It then dispatches the instructions to the respective execution units for execution. In a single cycle, the following mix of instructions can be dispatched simultaneously:

- One branch instruction (to the branch processor)

- One condition instruction (to the branch processor)

- One fixed-point instruction (to the FXU)

- One floating-point instruction (to the FPU)

It can be seen that a CPU based on the POWER architecture has a potential throughput of four instructions per clock cycle. This concept of dispatching multiple instructions per cycle to multiple execution units is called *superscalar design*.

An important concept in the design of the POWER architecture is the concept of *zero-cycle branching*. Traditionally, when a branch instruction directs the CPU to jump to a different section of the program code, the CPU wasted clock cycles getting the new target code from main memory while the execution units had no work to do. In the

POWER Architecture, the branch processor is implemented in the ICU. It looks ahead to the stream of instructions which the ICU fetches from main memory, takes out the branch instructions and executes them, and in a lot of cases (especially unconditional branches), it can cause the new target instructions to be fetched into the ICU in time to provide the FXU and FPU with an uninterrupted stream of instructions. This is termed zero-cycle branching.

The architecture also allows for schemes to perform branch prediction. Generally, these schemes use various methods to try and predict whether a conditional branch operation (for example, branch if A=B) will result in a branch or not. If the branch processor can get a correct prediction earlier, the instruction cache can fetch the necessary instructions from memory to feed the fixed-point and floating-point units with an uninterrupted stream of instructions to execute. Branch prediction schemes usually result in an improvement in execution time by reducing branch delay. Branch delay occurs when the instruction cache has to fetch instructions from a branch target area while the execution units are idle.

The set of instructions in the POWER Architecture was designed to have as much function as possible. This goes against the original spirit of RISC but the intent here is to optimize as much as possible the path length of programs. With more function in the instructions, fewer instructions are needed to do a piece of work. Chapter 3, "RISC versus CISC" on page 3-1 discusses this architectural decision and its bearing on the RISC versus CISC debate.

2.1.4 What Does All That Mean?

What aims do the various features of the POWER Architecture serve to achieve?

1. The instruction set was designed to optimize the *path length* of programs. This was one of the goals which would contribute to reducing instruction set cycles and hence execution time.

2. Multiple instructions can be dispatched and executed in the same clock cycle. This is aimed at reducing the *cycles per instruction* component. Together with objective number 1, the objective is to achieve *reduced instruction set cycles* which would in turn have a beneficial effect on execution time.

3. Zero-cycle branching also improves throughput and is aimed at reducing the cycles per instruction variable.

4. A tightly coupled FPU greatly improves performance for scientific and engineering applications. One important goal of designing the POWER Architecture was for it to effectively support both commercial and scientific environments.

2.2 Some General Concepts

The concepts and ideas below will help you to understand the various aspects of the PowerPC Architecture and their importance.

2.2.1 Pipelining and Superscalar Dispatch

Typical execution of a computer instruction requires a four-stage process:

1. *Instruction Fetch* involves fetching the instruction from main memory.

2. *Dispatch* or *Decode* is the process of decoding the instruction, getting the operands referred to in the instruction, and passing all these to the execution unit.

3. *Execution* involves the actual computation or execution of the instruction.

4. *Store* is the act of storing any results of the computation back into memory.

Each stage can be considered as taking up one CPU cycle. Of course, in a real implementation, different types of instructions go through different variations of the four-stage process and some of the stages may take more than one CPU cycle. But for ease of explanation, we can generalize here and say that there is a four-stage process with each stage using up one CPU cycle.

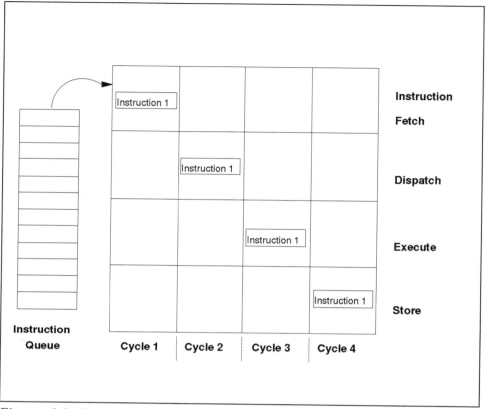

Figure *2-3. The Instruction Execution Process without Pipelining*

Figure 2-3 shows how an instruction is processed through the four stages. This process achieves a throughput of one instruction every four cycles; that is, one instruction is completely processed every four cycles. We can see that this scheme can be easily made more efficient. While the instruction is going through one stage, the rest of the four stages are lying idle and not doing any work. This brought about the idea of pipelining.

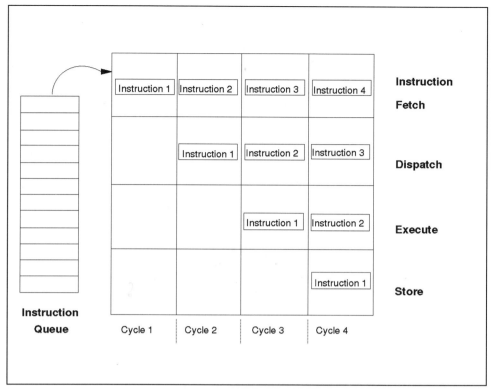

Figure   2-4. Basic Pipelining

Figure 2-4 shows the four-stage process with simple pipelining implemented. This is a much more efficient scheme than the previous one. While one stage is processing an instruction, the other stages move on to the next instruction in the stream, like an assembly line. In this way, we can potentially achieve a throughput of one instruction per cycle.

Basic pipelining by itself can improve the performance of the instruction execution process. But the POWER and PowerPC Architectures scale this performance improvement even further with superscalar instruction dispatch. Superscalar design essentially adds one more dimension to pipelining.

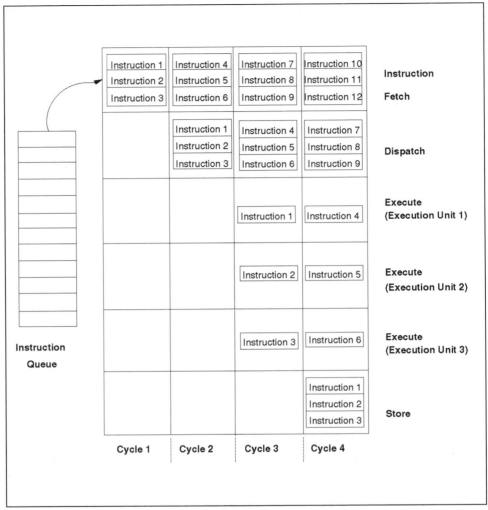

Figure 2-5. Pipelining with Superscalar Instruction Dispatch

Figure 2-5 illustrates how the instruction execution process works with superscalar dispatch. There can be any number of independent execution units, but here we show an implementation with three execution units. Since up to three instructions can be executed in parallel, three instructions can be fetched every cycle. These instructions will be dispatched to the three execution units in parallel. If the execution units can be fed with an uninterrupted stream of instructions, such an implementation can achieve a potential throughput of three instructions per cycle.

The concepts explained above show how the PowerPC Architecture uses multiple parallel execution units and multiple instruction dispatch to achieve improved throughput.

2.2.2 Load/Store Architecture

Traditionally, RISC architectures used the load/store method of working with data instead of the large number of addressing modes favored by CISC architectures.

Instructions in CISC architectures usually have a large variety of addressing modes to specify the data which they are referring to (a discussion of these addressing modes are beyond the scope of this book). In an instruction that performs a computation on data, the data is usually referred to directly in their memory location using any one of the addressing modes.

Instructions in RISC architectures tended to have only a few modes of addressing data. In addition, when operations are performed on data, the data is usually first *loaded* into CPU registers. The computation is performed on the data in the registers and the results are then *stored* back into memory.

As an example, the instruction:

```
A = B + C
```

in a CISC architecture will be translated by a compiler in a RISC architecture to:

```
LOAD B into R1
LOAD C into R2
R3 = R1 + R2
STORE R3 into A
```

where A, B, C are locations of data in main memory and R1, R2, R3 are registers.

This method of moving all data between registers and main memory and only performing operations on data in the registers is called *load/store architecture*. The instructions that move data between the registers and main memory are called load/store instructions.

2.2.3 Cache Coherency and Snooping

Cache memory is high-speed memory that is used as a buffer between the CPU and main memory to speed up memory accesses. It is used because it is much faster than main memory. In all execution cycles, the CPU has to access memory at least once to fetch instructions. Usually, it has to access memory a few more times to fetch and store operands. In this way, memory access speed became a bottleneck to CPU performance because memory speed was far slower compared to CPU speed. One solution then was to build a high-speed buffer between the CPU and main memory. This buffer was built using more expensive technology than main memory but was also faster than main memory. This buffer, called cache, works because of what is known as the *principle of locality*. Whenever the CPU fetches an instruction or piece of data from memory, it takes what it wants word by word. A word is usually a two to four byte piece of data depending on the architecture. But when a CPU fetches something from memory, there is a good chance that the next piece of data it needs will be somewhere near the piece that was read earlier. This is the principle of locality.

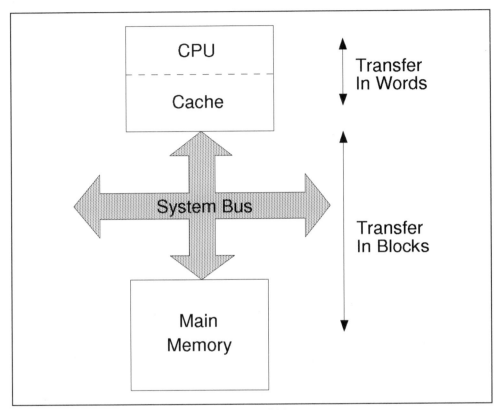

Figure 2-6. *Data Transfer Between CPU And Memory*

Figure 2-6 shows how cache memory takes advantage of the principle of locality to speed up memory accesses. When the CPU does a memory reference, entire blocks of data are brought into cache. These blocks can contain many bytes of data, maybe three or four times what the CPU actually needs. There is a good chance that the next piece of data that the CPU wants to access is in this block and already in the cache. Usually, if the data is to be updated by the CPU, the copy that is in cache is modified.

Cache memory is used widely today in CPU implementations to improve performance. But complications can arise in the case of multiprocessing.

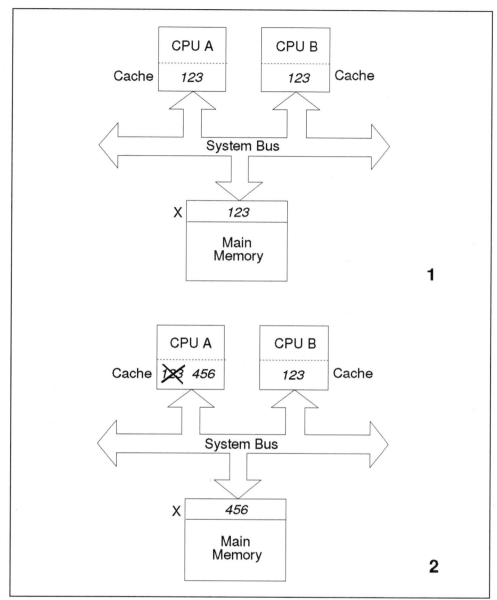

Figure   2-7. An Incoherent View of Memory

Figure 2-7 shows what can happen in a multiprocessor implementation. In a multiprocessor environment, a few CPUs, each with its own cache, share a single stack of main memory.

1. CPUs A and B are processing different instructions but it just happens that at some point in time they need data from the location in memory called X. X currently has a value of 123. So, X is brought into the caches of CPUs A and B.

2. Now, CPU A performs some operation that changes the value of X to 456 and writes out this value to main memory. We can see that A and B now have an *incoherent view* of memory; that is, their views of what X should be do not tally with each other.

   Imagine what would happen if CPU B wanted to perform an arithmetic operation on X. It would be using the wrong value of X!

This is just a simple example to show what can possibly happen. There are many other possible scenarios which can occur. The term *cache coherency* is used to describe the situation when multiple caches sharing main memory agree with each other on what is in memory; that is, they all have an accurate view of memory. It is very important to put in techniques to ensure cache coherency when designing the cache subsystem. *Snooping* is one such technique.

The problem with the cache incoherency scenario above is that the individual caches are not aware of what each other are doing. If they were allowed to "see" what all the caches are doing, they could take the necessary action to maintain coherency. Bus snooping is a technique that allows them to do this.

When bus snooping is implemented, the caches keep a close watch on the activity going on along the system bus. In the scenario above, CPU B would have detected CPU A writing out the new value of X. It would have taken action to mark its own copy of X as being invalid. There are many other scenarios of incoherency that can arise and various other ways that bus snooping prevents incoherency. The important principle to keep in mind is that all the caches that share memory must watch the bus activity and take action accordingly to maintain coherency.

2.2.4 Cache Write Through and Write Back Policies

Now, think of what would happen if in the example shown in Figure 2-7 on page 2-13, CPU A did not write the new value of X out to memory immediately.

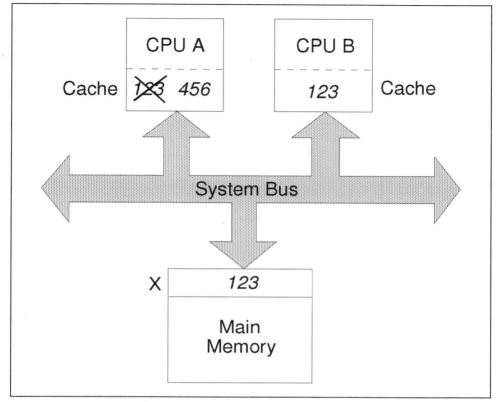

Figure   2-8. *No Immediate Write Back*

Figure 2-8 shows what happens in this case. Even if bus snooping were implemented, CPU B would not know that the value of X is changed because there is no activity on the system bus. This introduces two new concepts of cache behavior - *write through* and *write back*. These are policies that can be implemented to control the behavior of the cache system.

A write through policy states that any copy of data in cache that is modified by the CPU must be written out to memory immediately. This ensures that any changes to data in cache are always reflected in main memory as soon as possible. In addition, writing out of modified data generates system bus activity, which is useful for other caches that are snooping the bus. The disadvantage with this policy is the fact that any modification of data always requires movement of data to main memory. This takes time, generates additional bus traffic, and is not always necessary.

A write back policy is intended to overcome the main disadvantage of the write through policy. The write back method states that modified data can be kept in cache. It should be written to main memory when it is known that another processor is accessing or wants to access that piece of data in memory. In this way, modified data is only written out to memory when it is necessary.

2.2.5 Physical and Logical Memory

Main memory in most modern computer architectures are usually organized into small fixed size partitions. These partitions are called *pages*. The typical size of a page of memory is 2KB or 4KB.

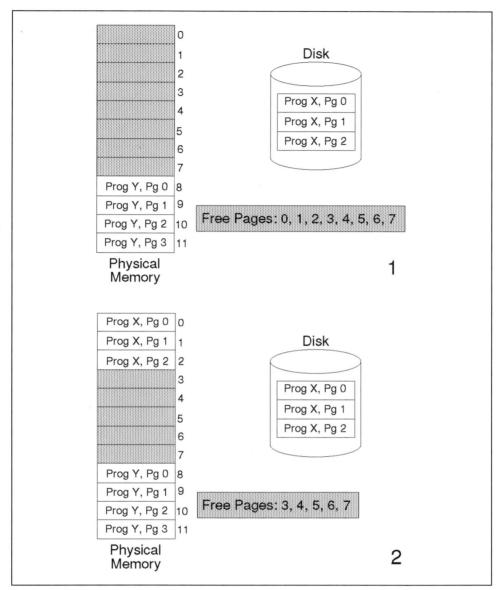

Figure   *2-9.*   *Program Loading into Memory*

Figure 2-9 shows how a program is loaded into memory.

1. Program X, which occupies three pages, is to be loaded into memory. The program is stored on disk. There is a list of pages which are not occupied in memory. Program Y is already in memory, occupying four pages.

2. The three pages of Program X are loaded into three free pages in memory.

The pages that are loaded into memory contain instructions and data for Program X. There will be addresses in the code to refer to data and branch target locations. But Program X may not be loaded into the same location in memory every time. For example, next time, pages 0, 1 and 2 may be occupied by some other program and X may have to be loaded into pages 4, 5 and 6. The addresses in the program will have to be changed every time the program is loaded! How are addresses specified in the program so that wherever it is loaded, the addresses still point accurately at the correct locations?

The problem is solved by using two types of addresses - *logical addresses* and *physical addresses*. Logical addresses are used within a program to refer to other locations within the program. It is expressed as a *displacement* relative to the beginning of a program. When a program is loaded into memory, the physical address of the beginning of the program is called the *base address*. While the program is being executed, the CPU converts the logical addresses in memory into physical addresses. This process is called *address translation*. Address translation is done by adding the base address of the program to the logical addresses. Figure 2-10 illustrates the difference between logical and physical addresses.

Program	Logical Address	Physical Address
	0	Base Address
	1	Base Address + 1
	2	Base Address + 2
	3	Base Address + 3
	4	Base Address + 4
	5	Base Address + 5
	6	Base Address + 6

Figure 2-10. Physical and Logical Addresses

In the examples so far, the programs have been loaded into memory into pages that are directly next to each other, or *contiguous pages*. In Figure 2-9 on page 2-17, the memory subsystem could find three free contiguous pages in which to load Program X. What would happen if there are not enough free contiguous pages in memory, as shown in Figure 2-11?

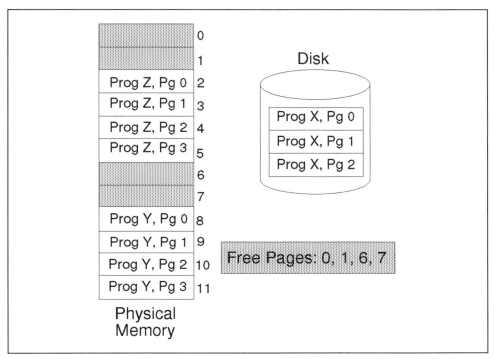

Figure *2-11. Allocation of Free Pages*

One thing the memory subsystem could do is *compact* the memory. This involves rearranging the programs in memory such that all the free pages are together in one block. But to do this involves a lot of effort and time spent by the CPU.

A more popular method is to place the pages of the program wherever there are free pages in memory. There is no need to place them in contiguous locations. The operating system keeps track of where the pages are by maintaining a *page table*.

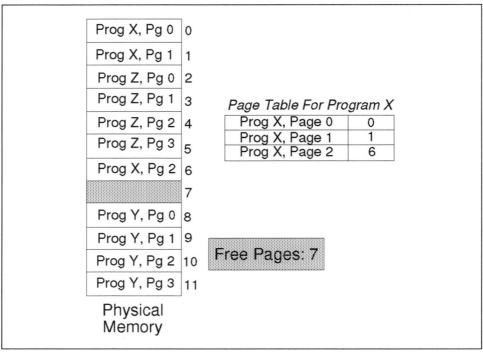

Figure *2-12.* *Tracking Page Allocation with Page Tables*

Figure 2-12 shows how Program X can be loaded without having to put it into contiguous pages of memory. A page table is maintained for X showing the pages and where they are kept in memory. By maintaining page tables like this for all the programs, pages can be loaded anywhere in memory.

2.2.6 Virtual Memory and Demand Paging

Physical memory is relatively expensive to implement compared to fixed disks. Typically, the amount of real memory installed in modern personal computers amount to no more than tens of megabytes. Fixed disk sizes are typically hundreds of megabytes or even gigabytes.

Virtual memory is a means of using the cheaper fixed disk space to overcome the limits of more expensive real memory. It allows the computer to appear to have more memory than actually installed.

At any instant, execution of program code is confined to only a small section of the total program. Only the few pages of instructions and data that the CPU uses at that instant is actually needed in memory. Virtual memory gives the program the illusion of having a very large memory space. But only the few pages that the CPU uses at any instant is loaded into real memory. The rest of the pages stay on the fixed disk.

When the CPU needs some more pages of code and these pages are not in memory, they are brought in from disk. This gives rise to the term *demand paging*, which means that pages are only brought into memory when it is needed, or demanded, by the CPU. The principle of locality, mentioned earlier in 2.2.3, "Cache Coherency and Snooping" on page 2-11, ensures the probability that the CPU will only need a few pages of code for a period of time. This results in acceptable performance most of the time, as pages brought into memory can satisfy the CPU's requests for a while before some more pages must be loaded.

In this way, programs can use a very large memory space - perhaps hundreds of megabytes or a few gigabytes. But the amount of real memory is much smaller than that. In fact, even the size of a single program can be larger than real memory.

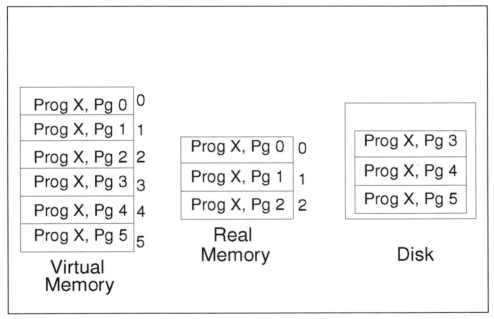

Figure 2-13. *Virtual Memory and Swapping*

Figure 2-13 gives an example of how a program larger than the size of real memory can be stored during execution. Assume that the size of the program is six pages and the size of real memory only three pages. When the program begins to execute, the first page is brought from disk storage into real memory. When more pages need to be accessed by the CPU, they are brought into real memory from disk. Meanwhile, the other pages reside on the disk. When all the pages in real memory are filled up and another page is needed in memory, one of the pages that are already in real memory will be *swapped out*. The process of swapping out involves:

1. Deciding which page in real memory to swap out

2. Writing it back to disk if anything in the page was modified

3. Bringing in the new page that is needed

2.2.7 Big- and Little-Endian Memory Organization

Data is accessed by programs in data types of different sizes. For example, character strings are accessed in individual bytes. Numbers such as integers can be in 32-bit words. Floating-point operands can be in 32-bit words or 64-bit *double words*.

These data are stored in memory and accessed in bytes. In the case of operands that are more than one byte in size, the CPU expects the bytes to be in a certain order when fetching the data. There are generally two ways of organizing the bytes in memory. One is called *Big-Endian* byte ordering and the other is *Little-Endian* byte ordering.

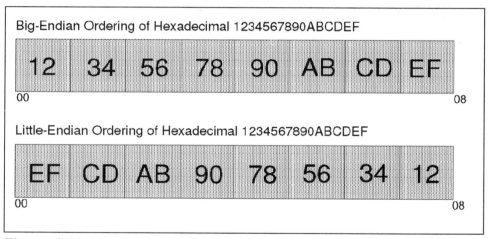

Figure 2-14. Big- and Little-Endian Byte Ordering

In Big-Endian ordering, the data is stored starting with the most significant byte and ending with the least significant. The order is reversed in Little-Endian organization. Figure 2-14 gives an example of how the hexadecimal number *1234567890ABCDEF* (a 64-bit double word) is stored in memory in Big-Endian and Little-Endian organizations.

Traditionally, computer architectures and operating systems are designed to support one of the byte orders. So, an operating system written to support Little-Endian byte ordering would not be able to run on a CPU built to support Big-Endian byte-ordering.

2.3 The PowerPC Architecture

The definition of the PowerPC Architecture provides a basic conceptual model that provides many degrees of freedom for various implementations of the architecture to suit different needs. This flexibility was one of the important design goals for the architecture. This and other design criteria will be outlined in the next section. Next, the layers of the architecture and the basic processor model will be examined.

2.3.1 Design Goals of the PowerPC Architecture

The PowerPC Architecture was designed with the following goals in mind:

- The architecture should maintain application binary compatibility with the POWER Architecture. This would enable PowerPC-based machines to leverage on the existing base of RISC System/6000 applications and users. As a result, the PowerPC instruction set and programming model is similar to the one for the POWER Architecture.

- The architecture definition should allow flexibility and variety in implementation to meet the requirements of different target markets and uses. It was the intention of the designers to make the PowerPC an effective platform for a wide range of implementations, from hand-held devices to powerful mainframe-style machines. This has been achieved in the design in a number of ways:

  1. Software and hardware can play variable roles in different implementations. For example, although the basic conceptual model includes a tightly coupled FPU (like the POWER Architecture), floating-point operations can be implemented in software instead of a hardware FPU. This will be useful for lowering cost in machines where floating-point performance is not important. The architecture definition is not rigid in these cases and it makes for a much more flexible architecture.

  2. The layered definition described in 2.3.2, "Levels of PowerPC Architecture" on page 2-24 above provides the PowerPC Architecture with much of its flexibility. Implementations need not comply with all the layers of the architecture.

  3. Implementers can add their own instructions, registers or exceptions which are specific to their requirements. This can allow, for example, special-purpose devices to be built which use instructions and registers not found in the normal PowerPC instruction set and programming model.

  4. Many hardware-specific details are not prescribed by the PowerPC architecture or are only described in a very general sense. For example, the bus signals are not specified. The size and type of cache and whether there should be separate instruction and data caches is not specified. It is also not specified which execution units should execute which instructions.

It can be seen that there are many degrees of freedom for implementations which optimize the basic PowerPC Architecture to suit various uses.

- The PowerPC Architecture should provide support for both uniprocessor and multiprocessor systems. The storage control subsystem of the PowerPC Architecture has been designed to support multiprocessing.

- The architecture should support 64-bit instruction operation in the future while providing upward compatibility for the current 32-bit architecture. To achieve this aim, a set of 64-bit extensions were defined that ensures software compatibility between the current 32-bit architecture and the next generation of 64-bit processors. Implementations can comply with either the base 32-bit architecture or the extended 64-bit architecture.

2.3.2 Levels of PowerPC Architecture

The PowerPC Architecture consists of different layers. Adherence to the PowerPC Architecture can be measured according to which of the following levels of the architecture is implemented:

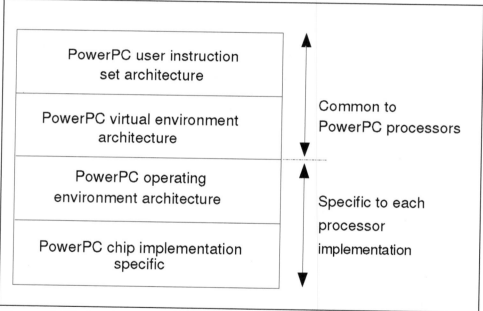

Figure   2-15. *Levels of the PowerPC Architecture*

2.4.1.1 Instruction Set

The following categories of instructions are defined in the PowerPC architecture:

- *Integer instructions*

  These instructions operate on integer operands. They include instructions that perform arithmetic on integer operands and instructions that perform logical operations (such as negating a number). Examples include:

  - Integer arithmetic instructions

  - Integer compare instructions

  - Integer logical instructions

  - Integer rotate and shift instructions

- *Floating-point instructions*

  These instructions operate on floating-point numbers. Examples include:

  - Floating-point arithmetic instructions

  - Floating-point multiply-add instructions (of the form A+BxC)

  - Floating-point compare instructions

- *Load/Store instructions*

  These instructions are used to move data between main memory and CPU registers and are necessary to support the load/store character of the PowerPC Architecture.

  Note that the order in which data is actually transferred from memory may not be the same as the program order because of caching. For example, if the two instructions:

  ```
  Load X into R1
  Load Y into R2
  ```

  (where X, and Y are locations in memory, and R1 and R2 are registers) are in program order, the second one may complete first if Y is already in cache and X is not. This could cause difficulties if programs needed data to be loaded in a certain order. This can be solved by *memory synchronization* instructions which are under the category of processor control instructions.

  The set of load/store instructions includes:

  - Integer load and store instructions

  - Floating-point load and store instructions

- *Flow control instructions*

  These are instructions that affect the instruction flow. They include branch instructions and logical operations on the condition register.

- *Memory control instructions*

  This set of instructions can be used for control of the cache subsystem and other aspects of the memory subsystem. There is a small group of cache control instructions in this set which can be used by user-level programs. These instructions allow programs to pre-load into cache the next set of data while processing the current set. This overlapping of loading and processing may be used by programs to improve efficiency and execution time.

- *Processor control instructions*

  This is a group of mostly supervisor-level instructions that allow access to special control registers. These registers control the operation of the processor and generally a certain level of privilege is required to access these registers.

  Another set of instructions in this category allow synchronization of memory accesses. As mentioned earlier in the load/store instructions category, memory access synchronization is sometimes necessary to maintain a certain order when accessing data. Synchronization instructions help to maintain the correct program order. Using synchronization instructions, the example given in the section on load/store instructions can be rewritten as:

  ```
  Load X into R1
  Synchronize
  Load Y into R2
  ```

  The *synchronize* instruction will ensure that all outstanding memory accesses are completed.

PowerPC instructions have the following attributes:

- All instructions are of a fixed-length (32-bits) and consistent format. This allows the instruction decoding mechanism to be kept simple and efficient. An efficient decoding system permits easier implementation of pipelining and superscalar dispatch.

- Integer instructions operate on byte, half-word and word operands (a word in the PowerPC Architecture is defined as 32-bits).

- Floating-point instructions operate on either single-precision (one word) or double-precision (double word) floating-point operands.

- Instructions that perform computation do not work directly on operands in memory. The PowerPC Architecture uses the load/store method of working with data. Operands must be loaded from memory to registers using load instructions, worked on and then, if modified, stored back to memory using store instructions.

- Instructions use a non-destructive format when working with operands. Normally, computational instructions are of the form *R1 = R2 operation R3*. This ensures that operands in the registers R2 and R3 are not destroyed by the computation.

2.4.1.2 Addressing Modes

Addresses are used in instructions to specify the location of operands in memory. They are used by the CPU to tell the memory subsystem where to get the data. An addressing mode is a method of specifying the address of an operand. There is more than one addressing mode and computer architectures usually employ a few.

The PowerPC Architecture specifies two basic and very simple addressing modes. Both methods use a base address, taken from a register and a displacement. The two values are added together to produce the 32-bit *effective address*. The effective address is what the CPU presents to the memory subsystem to locate the data. The two addressing modes differ on the source from which the displacement is taken.

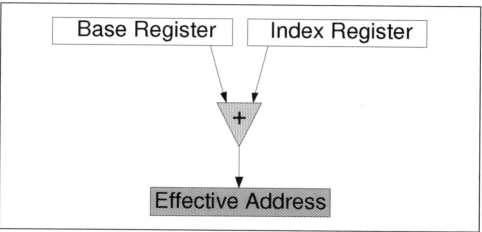

Figure 2-17. Register Index Addressing Mode

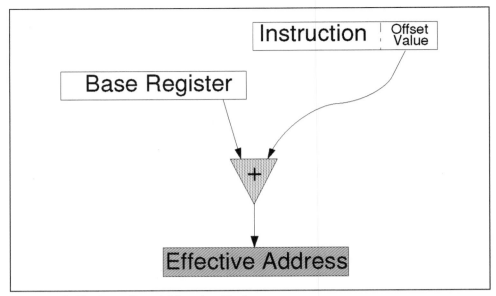

Figure   2-18. *Immediate Addressing Mode*

- *Register Index*

  Effective Address = Base Register + Index Register

- *Immediate Addressing*

  Effective Address = Base Register + Offset Value

The offset value in immediate addressing is specified directly in the instruction.

Note that because of the load/store characteristic of the PowerPC architecture, these addressing modes are not used in a computational instruction to address operands. Instead, they are used in load/store instructions to refer to memory locations to put/take data. They are also used in branch instructions to refer to target locations for branching.

2.4.2 PowerPC Programming Model

This section starts by discussing the PowerPC register set - what registers are available for programs that run on the PowerPC Architecture and what are their functions. We will then take a brief look at the types of data storage organization supported by the PowerPC Architecture.

2.4.2.1 PowerPC Register Set

This section looks at the register set defined by the PowerPC architecture and the functions of some of the register sets.

The programming model defines 32 general-purpose registers (GPRs), 32 floating-point registers (FPRs), some special-purpose registers (SPRs), and a few other miscellaneous registers.

PowerPC processors operate at two privilege levels - supervisor level and user level. The supervisor mode of operation is typically used by the operating system or extensions to the operating system. The user mode of operation is usually used by user-level applications. Having different levels of privileges allows the operating system to control the environment while protecting critical system resources from being misused.

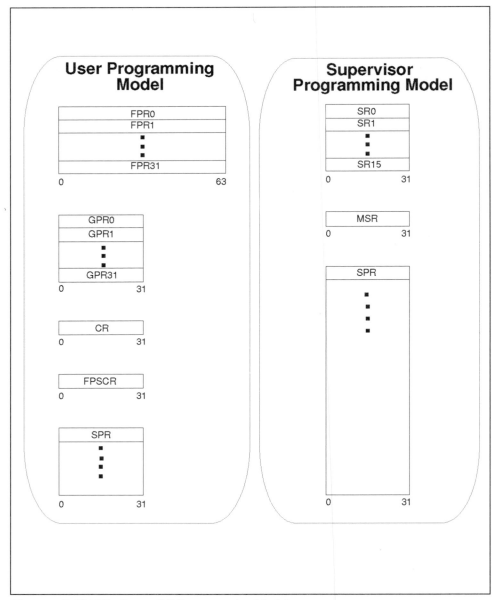

Figure   2-19. The PowerPC Programming Model

Figure 2-19 shows the register set in the PowerPC programming model and the division
between the supervisor and user programming models. Some of the registers defined in
the architecture are:

- *General-Purpose Registers*

  GPRs are used as user-level, general-purpose data registers. They are 32 bits wide in a 32-bit PowerPC implementation and 64 bits wide in a 64-bit implementation. The programming model defines a set of 32 such registers.

- *Floating-Point Registers*

  There are 32 64-bit FPRs defined in the model. These registers serve as data source or target registers for floating-point computations.

- *Condition Register (CR)*

  The CR is a 32-bit user-level register that contains eight 4-bit fields. These fields reflect the results of certain operations, such as integer and floating-point, compare and arithmetic computations. These fields are accessed using condition register instructions for testing and conditional branching.

- *Floating-Point Status And Control Register (FPSCR)*

  This register contains fields that show information on floating-point computations. Some of the fields can be set by user-level programs to control the behavior of floating-point operations (for example, how much rounding should be performed on floating-point numbers).

- *Machine State Register (MSR)*

  The MSR is a critical supervisor-level register. The fields in the register define the state of the processor. Examples of these fields include whether the processor is operating in user or supervisor mode and whether the CPU is handling an exception or performing normal processing.

- *Segment Registers (SRs)*

  The entire map of logical memory is divided into sixteen 256MB partitions. Each partition is called a segment. The 16 segments are identified by the 16 SRs.

- *Special-Purpose Registers (SPRs)*

  The programming model defines numerous SPRs. Some of these can be accessed at the user level while most require supervisor privileges. SPRs serve a variety of functions, ranging from indicating status and allowing the operating system to control and configure the system to performing special operations. Besides the SPRs defined in the basic model, PowerPC implementations can add on additional SPRs to perform special functions.

2.4.2.2 Bi-Endian Support

The PowerPC Architecture supports both Big- and Little-Endian modes of data storage. PowerPC implementations should be able to run in both Big- and Little-Endian modes *(but not both at the same time)*. This means that potentially any operating system, whether it operates in Big- or Little-Endian mode, should be portable to a PowerPC machine.

When a PowerPC system is first started up, it operates in Big-Endian mode by default. At that point, an operating system can switch the system to Little-Endian mode if needed. The architecture defines a 2-bit field in the MSR that specifies whether the system is operating in Big- or Little-Endian mode. The mode can be changed by changing the contents of the field. Note that PowerPC processors may implement a different way of mode switching. For example, the PowerPC 601 implements the mode switch in another 601-specific SPR called the HID0 instead of the MSR.

The PowerPC Reference Platform contains a specification of the Endian-mode switching process for operating systems.

2.4.3 PowerPC Memory Model

The memory model defines the size and attributes of addressable memory, how memory is managed and the cache architecture.

2.4.3.1 How Memory Is Partitioned

The 32-bit PowerPC Architecture allows up to 2^{32} bytes (4GB) of logical address space. The virtual address space is 2^{52} bytes. This means that logical addresses are 32 bits wide and virtual addresses are 52 bits wide.

The 64-bit architecture allows for 2^{64} bytes of logical address space and 2^{80} bytes of virtual memory.

The logical address space is divided into *segments* of 256MB. Each segment is divided into *pages* of 4KB.

A mechanism called *block address translation* (BAT) gives quick address translation for specially defined *blocks* in memory. These blocks are defined as entries in BAT registers which are part of the set of SPRs. The blocks can be set to be between 128KB and 256MB in size. Blocks are special areas in memory which may be frequently accessed. Examples are areas in memory representing some I/O devices or graphics devices. They are specially defined to allow for faster address translation. Figure 2-20 on page 2-37 illustrates how memory is partitioned.

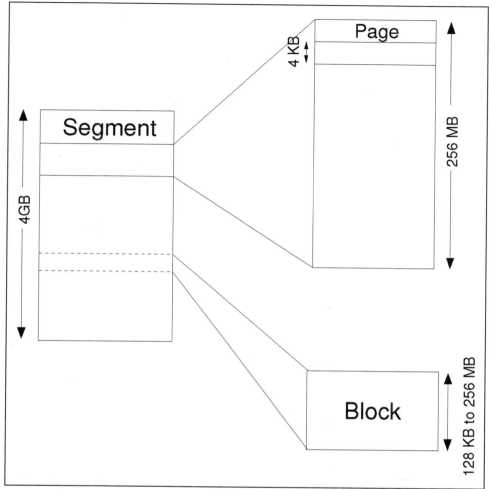

Figure 2-20. *How Memory Is Partitioned*

2.4.3.2 How the Partitions Are Accessed

2.4.2.1, "PowerPC Register Set" on page 2-32 described a set of segment registers. Each of these registers store the location of one segment. Page tables store the locations of pages, with each entry in the table (called a *page table entry* or PTE) storing the location of one page. Entries in a BAT register store the location of a block.

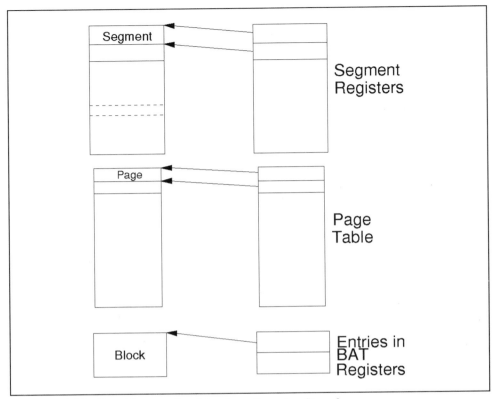

Figure *2-21.* *How Memory Partition Locations Are Stored*

Figure 2-21 shows where the locations of the various memory partitions are stored.

2.4.3.3 Memory Protection

Various areas of memory contain code and data for many programs, both at user and supervisor levels. Some areas of memory represent I/O devices - programs access the devices by using the addresses of these areas of memory. This is called *memory-mapped I/O*.

All these areas must be protected from unauthorized or invalid accesses by other programs. The job of enforcing this protection lies with the *memory management unit* (MMU). Memory areas can be protected either at the page or block partition level.

Pages are protected by fields in the page table entry. There is one PTE for each page and these entries contain some special fields that describe the page. One of the fields is for page access protection. The following levels of protection can be set for a page:

Table 2-2. *Page Access Protection Levels*

Protection Level	Supervisor-Level Programs		User-level Programs	
	Read	Write	Read	Write
Supervisor-only	Yes	Yes	No	No
Supervisor Write-only	Yes	Yes	Yes	No
Supervisor/User	Yes	Yes	Yes	Yes
Read-only	Yes	No	Yes	No

Table 2-2 shows the various levels of protection which can be set in the PTE and what it means to supervisor- and user-level programs. Note that wherever user-level programs are allowed to access a page, by default access is allowed to supervisor-level programs too. In fact, any page that is accessible by user-level programs *must* offer at least the same level of access by supervisor programs.

Blocks are protected by setting fields in the BAT register entries. Since each entry defines one block, each block can be configured as accessible by user or supervisor-level programs.

2.4.3.4 Address Translation

The MMU's primary responsibility is to translate logical addresses to physical addresses. Address translation is needed in the following events:

- Instruction accesses

  This occurs when the CPU needs instructions fetched from memory.

- Data accesses

  Data accesses to memory are generated by load and store instructions. This category includes I/O accesses that use memory-mapped I/O. As we recall, memory-mapped I/O allows programs to access I/O devices by using normal load/store instructions and addressing the device as if it were an area in memory.

  The address translation process for memory-mapped I/O is almost the same as that for normal data loads/stores to and from memory. The only difference is that, for memory-mapped I/O, the device must be accessed to get the data.

- *I/O controller interface accesses*

  This is an alternative way of accessing I/O devices. Messages are passed to and from the processor and the I/O controller for the device. This communication is used to provide control over the whole process as well as to transfer data. The messages are in the form of load/store instructions and *replies*, which are the messages that the I/O controller passes to the processor. I/O controller interface accesses are identified by a field in the segment register.

There are different address translation processes for the various types of memory partitions.

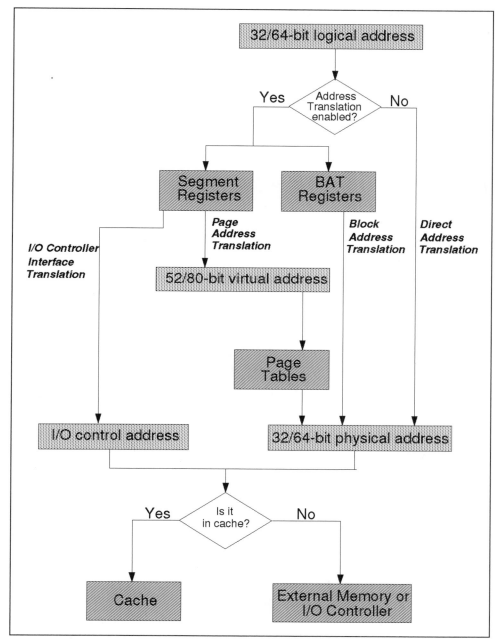

Figure **2-22.** *The Address Translation Process*

Figure 2-22 summarizes the various methods of address translation. There are basically four types of address translation processes:

- *Direct Address Translation*

  This is used if address translation is disabled. Address translation can be disabled by setting some bits in the machine state register (MSR). When translation is disabled, the logical address is used directly as the physical address.

- *Block Address Translation*

  In this process, the BAT registers are checked to see if the logical address refers to a defined block. If it does, the BAT register entry is used to generate a physical address.

- *Page Address Translation*

  The segment registers are used to generate the virtual address. The virtual page table is then accessed to map the virtual address to a physical address. This process is run in parallel with block address translation.

- *I/O Controller Interface Translation*

  When a field in the segment register indicates that it is an I/O controller interface access, page address translation is not used. Instead, the logical address is used to generate the messages that are used to communicate with the I/O controller.

  This process is also run in parallel with block address translation. If block address translation succeeds (that is, the address is in a defined block), *this process is ignored.*

After the physical address is generated, the cache unit is checked to see whether the requested code is in cache. If not, the address is put on the bus to access main memory or the I/O controller.

2.4.3.5 Cache Architecture

The PowerPC Architecture does not define the hardware aspects of cache implementations. It does not dictate whether there should be separate data and instruction caches or a unified cache. It does not restrict the size or organization of caches.

It does, however, define a method to control the caching of memory. This control works at the page and block levels. There are three bits known as the *W*, *I* and *M* bits (or collectively as WIM bits) in page table entries and BAT register entries. By setting or clearing WIM bits, the caching modes of that particular page or block can be controlled.

The bits have the following meanings:

- W bit - Write through/Write back

Setting the W bit means that the page or block follows a write through policy.

Clearing the W bit means that the page or block follows a write back policy.

- I bit - Cache Inhibition

Setting the I bit means that the page or block is *cache-inhibited*, that is, it is not to be cached at all. This is usually the case when the page or block represents an I/O device.

Clearing the I bit means that the page or block can be cached as normal.

- M bit - Coherency Control

When the M bit is set, coherency is enforced for the page or block. This involves the cache snooping discussed in 2.2.3, "Cache Coherency and Snooping" on page 2-11.

When the M bit is cleared, coherency is not enforced for that page or block.

Table 2-3 summarizes the WIM bit settings and what they mean. Note that when the I bit is set, caching is turned off and it does not matter what the W and M bits are set at.

Table 2-3.		*What the WIM Settings Mean*			
W	**I**	**M**	**Write through/Write back**	**Cache**	**Coherency**
0	0	0	Write back	On	No
0	0	1	Write back	On	Yes
1	0	0	Write through	On	No
1	0	1	Write through	On	Yes
X	1	X	-	Cache inhibited	-

2.4.4 PowerPC Exception Model

Exceptions are external signals, errors or unusual events that cause the CPU to switch to supervisor state. When the CPU is notified of an exception, it saves the state of the system in some registers and begins executing code found at some predefined location. This location is called an exception vector or exception handler. Exception handlers are defined for the types of exceptions which can be identified or foreseen. Exception vectors are executed in supervisor mode.

The various types of exceptions are defined by two characteristics - synchronous/asynchronous and precise/imprecise.

- *Synchronous* exceptions are caused by the instructions that the CPU is processing at a particular moment.

- *Asynchronous* exceptions are caused by external events or other conditions *not connected* to whatever the CPU is processing at the time that the exception occurred.

- *Precise* exceptions are exceptions where the exact cause of the exception is known and the machine state at the time of exception is known. They are usually recoverable.

- *Imprecise* exceptions are usually caused by a very serious failure or non-recoverable condition. They may cause the CPU to halt processing or stop execution of some program.

The combination of these two characteristics gives rise to four types of exceptions:

- *Synchronous, precise exceptions*

  These are exceptions caused by instructions. An example is an invalid address in the instruction. At the time these exceptions occur, the state of the machine is known. The CPU can save the state of the machine, handle the exception, and then continue with processing of other instructions.

- *Synchronous, imprecise exceptions*

  These are generally not supported in the PowerPC Architecture. Although there are some floating-point exceptions defined as synchronous imprecise in some implementations, they are handled as synchronous precise exceptions.

- *Asynchronous, precise exceptions*

  These are non-disastrous exceptions that are not caused by the instructions being processed by the CPU. Examples are external interrupts, which are signals from external devices to tell the CPU to handle something. A clock device may send signals to the CPU at regular intervals to keep time, for example.

- *Asynchronous, imprecise exceptions*

  An example of this type of exception is a system reset, which causes the CPU to stop processing, reset everything in the system and restart processing.

2.5 The PowerPC Processor Family

A PowerPC is a microprocessor designed to meet the standard developed by the alliance of IBM, Apple and Motorola. This standard specifies a common instruction-set architecture allowing to design and manufacture PowerPC processors, which then will be able to run the same code. The PowerPC Architecture is based on the POWER technology used in IBM's RS/6000 systems.

PowerPC Architecture and achieves its performance through concurrent execution of up to three instructions per cycle in its three parallel execution units:

- The fixed point unit
- The floating point unit
- The branch processing unit

The PowerPC 601 microprocessor clocks at speeds of up to 100MHz. At 66MHz, its estimated 60 SPECint92 and 80 SPECfp92 make it an excellent high-performance, low-cost solution for desktop systems. A detailed description of the PowerPC 601 microprocessor is given in 2.6.1, "The PowerPC 601" on page 2-48.

2.5.2 The PowerPC 603

The PowerPC 603 microprocessor is a 32-bit implementation, intended for use in uniprocessor applications, such as notebook computers and low-end desktop computers. High performance is achieved through concurrent execution of up to three instructions in five parallel execution units:

- The fixed point unit
- The floating point unit
- The branch processing unit
- The system unit
- The load/store unit

The Power PC 603 microprocessor incorporates low-power design and power management features to offer competitive advantage in cost sensitive and portable applications. 2.6.2, "The PowerPC 603" on page 2-54 describes the PowerPC 603 microprocessor in detail.

2.5.3 The PowerPC 604

The PowerPC 604 microprocessor is designed to deliver exceptional performance for high-end desktop systems, midrange server and high-performance graphics workstations. It is a superscalar, multiprocessor enabled chip that issues four instructions in parallel every clock cycle to six execution units. Its three stage double precision floating point unit allows the end user to take advantage of increasingly graphics oriented software packages, as well as multimedia applications, providing tremendous performance capabilities that were previously available only through expensive add-on hardware. 2.6.3, "The PowerPC 604" on page 2-60 describes the PowerPC 604 microprocessor in detail.

2.5.4 The PowerPC 620

The PowerPC 620 microprocessor is designed to deliver the maximum performance achievable with the current available half-micron CMOS process technology. This superscalar design implements the full 64-bit PowerPC architecture and includes an embedded L2 cache controller that interfaces to standard SRAM chips. The design is targeted at high-end desktop systems, workgroup server and transaction processing-based systems.

2.6 PowerPC Technology Details

We will now take a closer look at each of the processor implementations. We will briefly examine the internal processor architecture and focus on how it differs from the general PowerPC Architecture.

2.6.1 The PowerPC 601

The 601 processor probably differs from the general PowerPC architecture more than any other current implementation. This is due to its goal of being a "bridge" processor for the transition between POWER and PowerPC processor families. It allows most of the existing POWER applications to run unmodified. This gives application vendors time to recompile their software to take full advantage of the other PowerPC processors.

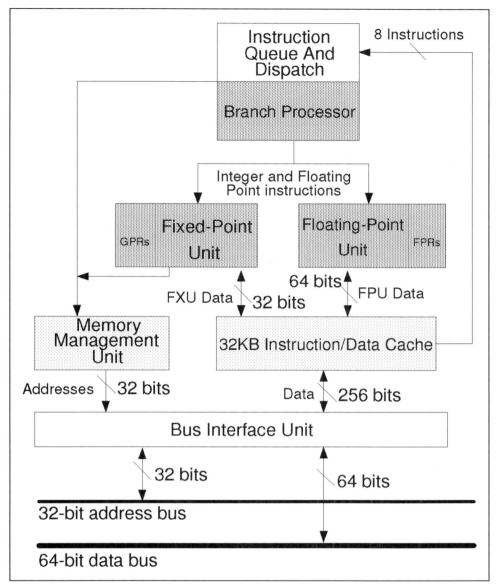

Figure **2-24.** *The PowerPC 601 Microprocessor Block Diagram*

Figure 2-24 shows the block diagram of the 601 processor. The various aspects of the processor architecture will be discussed next.

2.6.1.1 Instruction Queue and Dispatch Unit

The instruction unit (IU) contains an eight-instruction queue. Its job is to dispatch the instructions in the queue to the execution units in the CPU, as well as keep track of which instructions to fetch next.

The IU can fetch eight instructions per clock cycle from the cache. Eight instruction words is actually the size of a cache block. The large number of instructions that can be fetched each cycle offsets the 601's disadvantage of not having a separate instruction cache. To fetch the instructions, the IU generates the effective addresses of the instructions and hands them to the memory management unit.

The IU allows dispatch of integer instructions from the top four positions in the queue. Floating-point and branch instructions can be dispatched from the last four positions in the queue.

The IU benefits from the RISC attributes of the PowerPC instruction set: fixed-length instructions with simple format. This allows a simple fixed-length queue and easier decoding of instructions.

2.6.1.2 Branch Processor (BP)

The branch processor has an important job to perform. It constantly looks into the instruction queue, takes out the branch instructions and tries to predict whether the branch will be taken or not.

For conditional branches, the 601 architecture implements a mechanism called *static branch prediction*. When coding programs, the programmer can specify in the operand of a conditional branch whether or not the branch is likely to be taken. The BP works according to this "prediction". Branch prediction schemes generally improve the performance of the CPU when handling branch instructions.

The BP does its job by working with registers, such as the condition register (which was discussed in 2.4.2.1, "PowerPC Register Set" on page 2-32). These registers are implemented within the BP itself.

2.6.1.3 Fixed-Point Unit (FXU)

The FXU executes all the integer computation instructions which are dispatched to it by the IU. It has specialized units, such as a divider, a multiplier and an arithmetic logic unit, to perform this work. In addition, it has the responsibility of calculating effective or logical addresses for memory accesses. Any instruction that contains a memory address would require an address calculation by the FXU. This includes integer and floating-point load/store instructions. The FXU interfaces with the memory management unit to send out the logical addresses that have been calculated.

32-bit general-purpose registers (GPRs) are implemented in the FXU. These store the operands for integer computations.

2.6.1.4 Floating-Point Unit (FPU)

The FPU executes all the floating-point computations. It contains a multiply-add array which allows it to efficiently perform floating-point operations, such as add, multiply, divide and multiply-add.

The FPU also contains 32 64-bit floating-point registers (FPRs) as well as the floating-point status and control register (FPSCR). These registers were described in 2.4.2.1, "PowerPC Register Set" on page 2-32. The 601 FPU fully supports all the IEEE 754 data types in hardware.

2.6.1.5 Memory Management Unit (MMU)

The 601 is an implementation of the 32-bit PowerPC Architecture, which means that it supports up to 4 petabyte of virtual memory and 4 gigabyte of real memory. The MMU's job is to translate the logical addresses given to it by the FXU and BP to physical addresses which it presents to the cache unit. The address translation process works as outlined in 2.4.3.4, "Address Translation" on page 2-39. It has to be performed every time there is an instruction fetch or exchange of data between the CPU and memory.

The MMU makes use of *translation lookaside buffers* (TLBs) to do its job. TLBs are small, fast buffers that contain the most recent physical addresses that were translated. Because of the principle of locality, it is quite likely that an address that the MMU is looking for has just been translated recently. If it is found in the TLBs, the MMU just takes the physical address in the buffer. It does not have to go through the whole process of translation.

2.6.1.6 Cache Unit

The cache unit in the 601 is a 32KB unified instruction and data cache. It uses eight-way set associative mapping.

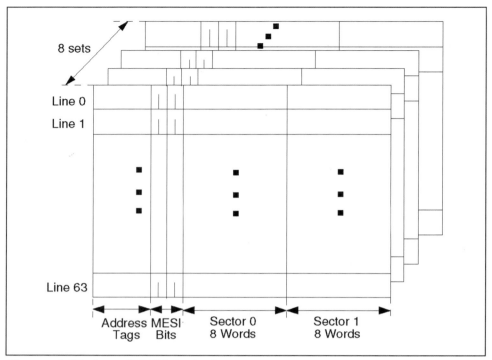

Figure **2-25.** *PowerPC 601 Cache Organization*

The cache is organized in eight sets of 64 lines. This operation is very efficient because a 601 cache line is the same size as eight instruction words. Each line contains the address tag, which is used to address and identify the contents of that line. Sixteen words of data can be stored on each line. This is divided into two sectors of eight words each. The sector is the cacheable unit in the 601 processor. This means that each sector can be individually loaded into the cache, flushed out from cache or marked as invalid.

When data is loaded from memory to cache, the words that the CPU is actually asking for are always transferred first, regardless of its position in the sector. After that the rest of the sector is transferred. This ensures that the cache unit can satisfy the CPU's request as fast as possible. This method of cache loading is called *critical word first*.

The cache unit is designed to follow a write back policy, but the 601 implements cache control using WIM bits as described in 2.4.3.5, "Cache Architecture" on page 2-42.

To enforce cache coherency in multiprocessor or multi-cache systems, the 601 cache unit uses snooping together with the MESI protocol. The MESI protocol uses 2 bits in the address tag lines to keep track of the state of a cache sector. This adds up to 4 bits per cache line. The 2 bits indicate which of the four states that the cache sector is in:

The CU uses a five-instruction buffer to make sure that instructions are completed in the proper order, despite the *out-of-order execution*.

2.6.2.8 Memory Management Units (MMUs)

The 603 implements two separate MMUs - the instruction MMU (I-MMU) and the data MMU (D-MMU). Each of the two MMUs work with the respective caches. As a 32-bit implementation of the PowerPC Architecture, the 603 supports up to 4 petabyte of virtual memory and 4 gigabytes of real memory.

The instruction unit performs the address calculation for instruction fetches and presents the effective addresses to the I-MMU. The LSU performs the address calculation for data loads and stores and presents the logical addresses to the D-MMU. The MMUs then translate the addresses to physical addresses and checks with the respective caches to see if the requested instructions or data are in cache. If not, external memory is accessed to bring in the required code or data.

Each MMU also has TLBs and BAT arrays implemented within the unit to speed up the work of address translation.

2.6.2.9 Cache Units

The 603 implements separate instruction and data caches. Each is 8KB in size and uses two-way set-associative mapping. Both caches are organized in a similar manner.

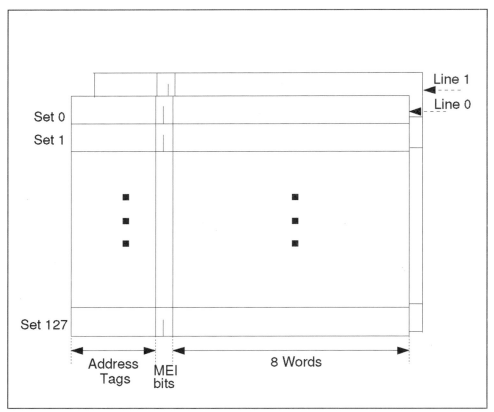

Figure   2-27. PowerPC 603 Data Cache Organization

Figure 2-27 shows the organization of a 603 data cache unit. The cache unit is divided into 128 sets of two lines each. Each line or block consists of 32 bytes or eight words, which is the cacheable unit. The line also contains an address tag and two state bits.

The two state bits implement the MEI protocol for cache coherency enforcement. The MEI protocol is similar to the MESI protocol described in 2.6.1.6, "Cache Unit" on page 2-51, except that there is no shared state. So the only states allowed are modified, exclusive and invalid.

The instruction cache unit is organized in a similar manner to the data cache - 128 sets of 2 lines, with each line holding eight words. The only difference is that, with the data cache, instead of two state bits, each line in the instruction cache has only one valid bit. The instruction cache is not snooped, and cache coherency must be enforced by software.

Cache loading transfers blocks of eight words at one time. This applies to both cache units. The eight-word block transfer is divided into four cycles of 64 bits each. The transfer is always performed with the critical double word first, that is, the two words actually required by the CPU are always transferred first regardless of their position in the cache line.

Snooping is implemented on the data cache but, unlike the 601 cache unit, it does not have a dedicated port for snooping. It has one port which is used for both data transfer and snooping.

2.6.2.10 Power Management
The 603 implements certain fields in the machine state register (MSR) that can select the power mode that the processor operates at. Software can manipulate these bits at supervisor-level to control the power mode settings.

There are four power-saving modes in the 603. The first three (doze, nap and sleep) progressively reduce the power consumed by the processor by disabling more and more functional units of the CPU. The fourth mode, called dynamic power management mode, minimizes power consumption during full operation. It does this by detecting any functional unit that is idle and putting this unit in a low-power state. This does not affect the operational performance or software execution process of the system.

2.6.2.11 Instruction Set
The 603 supports all the 32-bit PowerPC Architecture instructions in hardware.

2.6.2.12 Register Set
The 603 implements all the registers in the user-level programming model of the PowerPC Architecture. Some additional registers to help in the process of address translation are implemented in the supervisor-level SPR set of the 603.

2.6.2.13 Exception Model
The PowerPC 603 defines the following classifications of exceptions:

Table 2-6 (Page 1 of 2). 603 Microprocessor Exception Classifications		
	Precise	**Imprecise**
Synchronous	• Instruction-caused exceptions	None

Table 2-6 (Page 2 of 2). *603 Microprocessor Exception Classifications*

	Precise	**Imprecise**
Asynchronous	• External interrupt • Decrementer • System management exception • Soft system reset	• Machine check • Hard system reset

2.6.3 The PowerPC 604

The PowerPC 604 microprocessor features six different execution units:

- The branch processor execution unit
- Load/store execution unit
- Floating-point execution unit
- Three separate integer execution units
  - Two for all integer operations that can be executed in one single clock cycle and
  - one to execute all integer operations requiring more than one clock cycle

The PowerPC processor 604 can execute up to four instructions in one single clock cycle. The processor features zero-cycle capability as well as support for multiprocessing.

Figure 2-28 on page 2-61 shows a block diagram of the PowerPC 604 processor. The various components of the processor will be examined next.

These are software-accessible registers that provide detailed information concerning the dispatch, execution, completion, and memory access of the PowerPC instructions.

2.6.4 The PowerPC 620

The 620 is an implementation of the PowerPC family of RISC microprocessors. The 620 implements the PowerPC Architecture as it is specified for 64-bit addressing, which provides 64-bit effective (logical) addresses, integer data types of 8, 16, 32, and 64 bits, and floating-point data types of 32 and 64 bits (single and double precision). The 620 is software compatible with the 32-bit version of the PowerPC microprocessor family.

The 620 is a superscalar processor capable of issuing four instructions per cycle. As many as six instructions can finish execution at the same time. The 620 has six execution units:

- Floating-point unit
- Branch processing unit
- Load/store unit
- Three integer units
  - Two for all integer operations that can be executed in one single clock cycle
  - One to execute all integer operations requiring more than one clock cycle

Figure 2-30 on page 2-66 shows a block diagram of the PowerPC 620 processor. The various components of the processor will be examined next.

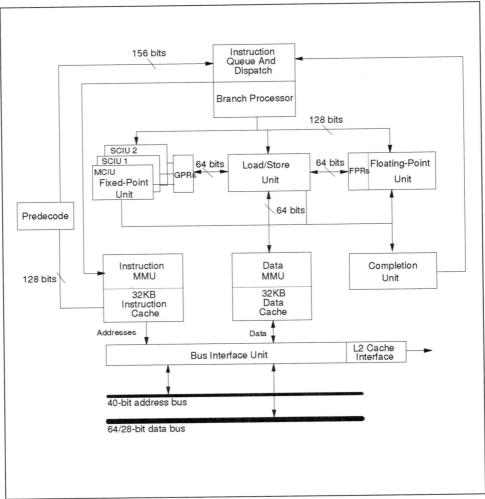

Figure 2-30. *The PowerPC 620 Microprocessor Block Diagram*

2.6.4.1 Instruction Queue "Fetch" and Dispatch

The instruction unit fetches up to four instructions per clock cycle from the instruction cache. Instructions for each of the execution units are dispatched from this queue.

2.6.4.2 Branch Processor Unit (BPU)

The BPU is similar to the one implemented in the 603. It looks into the stream of instructions fetched by the instruction unit, takes out the branch instructions and executes them. It makes use of branch prediction schemes to handle conditional branches. The BPU has its own set of registers to work with, including the condition register.

All branches, including unconditional branches, are placed in a reservation station until conditions are resolved and they can be executed. At that point branch instructions are executed in order; the completion unit is notified whether the prediction was correct.

2.6.4.3 Completion Unit (CU)

The CU retires executed instructions and updates register files and control registers. The CU can quickly remove instructions from a mispredicted branch, and the Branch Processor unit begins dispatching from the correct path. The CU guarantees a sequential programming model by monitoring all dispatched instructions and retiring them in order. The CU can retire several instructions per cycle.

2.6.4.4 Rename Buffers

To avoid contention for a given register location, the 620 provides rename registers for storing instruction results before the completion unit commits them to the architected register. Eight rename registers are provided for the GPRs, eight for the FPRs, and eight each for the condition register.

2.6.4.5 Fixed-Point Unit (FXU)

The 620 has three FXUs to improve cycle times. It has two single-cycle integer units (SCIU) and one multiple-cycle integer unit (MCIU). The one MCIU executes all integer instructions, such as integer multiply, divide, and all move to/from special-purpose registers. The two SCIUs execute all other register-to-register instructions in one cycle. Each SCIU and MCIU has one two-entry reservation station to minimize calls.

The 620 FXU has 32 general-purpose registers (GPR) for integer operands.

2.6.4.6 Floating-Point Unit (FPU)

The FPU implemented in the 620 as the one in the 603 is IEEE 754-1985 compliant for both single- and double-precision operations. It also supports non-IEEE mode for time-critical operations. The 620 FPU has a two-entry reservation station to minimize stalls and thirty-two 64-bit floating point registers (FPR).

2.6.4.7 Load/Store Unit (LSU)

The LSU implemented in the 620 is similar to the one in 603.

The LSU includes a 64-bit adder dedicated for EA calculations.

2.6.4.8 Memory Management Units (MMUs)

The MMUs implemented in the 620 are similar to the ones in 603 except that the 620 supports up to one heptabyte (2^{80}) of virtual memory and one terabyte (2^{40}) of physical memory.

2.6.4.9 Cache Units (L1)

The 620 implements separate instruction and data caches. Each is 32KB in size and uses eight-way set-associative mapping. Both caches are organized in a similar manner.

Figure 2-31 shows the organization of a 620 (L1) data cache unit.

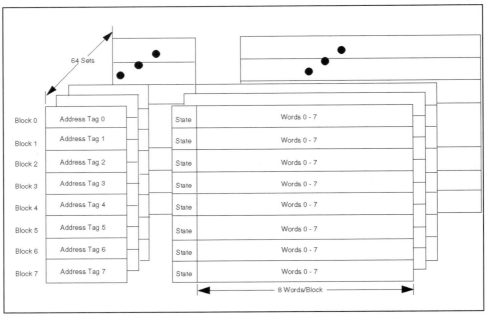

Figure 2-31. The PowerPC 620 (L1) Data Cache Organization

The parity checked cache unit is divided into 64 sets of eight lines each. Each line or block consists of 64 bytes or 16 words, which is the cachable unit. The line also contains an address tag and two state bits.

The two state bits implement the MESI protocol for cache coherency enforcement. (See 2.6.1.6, "Cache Unit" on page 2-51 for MESI details.)

The instruction cache unit is organized in a similar manner to the data cache: 64 sets of 8 lines, with each holding 16 words. The only difference is that, with the instructions cache, instead of two state bits, each line has only one valid bit. The instruction cache is not snooped, and cache coherency must be enforced by software.

Cache loading transfers blocks of 16 words at one time. This applies to both cache units. The transfer is always performed with the critical double word first, that is, the two words actually required by the CPU are always transferred first regardless of their position in the cache line.

The cache is programmable on a per page or per block basis for write back or write through. It can also be disabled or locked via software.

2.6.4.10 Level 2 Cache Interface (L2)

The 620 provides an integrated L2 cache controller that supports L2 configurations from 1MB to 128MB, using the same block size (64 bytes) as the internal cache (L1). The L2 cache is a direct mapped, error correction code (ECC) protected, unified instruction and data secondary cache that supports the use of single- and double-register synchronous static RAM.

2.6.4.11 Power Management

The 620 provides two power savings mode, called *NAP* mode and *DOZE* mode. Software initiates both *NAP* and *DOZE* mode by setting the MSR.

In the *DOZE* mode, all internal activity stops except for decrementer, time base, and interrupt logic and the 620 does not snoop bus activity unless the system asserts the WAKE-UP input signal

In the *NAP* mode, there is nothing in the caches subject to snoop activity. Assertion of the WAKE-UP signal will cause the 620 to awaken, process a snoop miss in the data cache, and return to the *NAP* mode.

2.6.4.12 Instruction Set

The 620 support all the 64-bit PowerPC Architecture instructions and most optional PowerPC instructions in hardware.

2.6.4.13 Register Set

The 620 implements all the registers in the user instruction set architecture (UISA), the virtual environment architecture (VEA) and the operating environment architecture (OEA) (ie. supervisor-level) plus some 620 specific registers, such as Performance Monitor and Cache Control.

2.6.4.14 Exception Model

The PowerPC 620 defines the following classification of exceptions:

Table 2-8. *620 Microprocessor Exception Classifications*

Type	Exception
Asynchronous/nonmaskable	• Machine check • System reset
Asynchronous/maskable	• External interrupt • Decrementer • System management interrupt (not defined by the PowerPC Architecture)
Synchronous / precise	Instruction-caused
Synchronous / imprecise	Floating-point

2.6.4.15 Performance Monitor

The 620 incorporates a performance monitor facility that designers can use to help bring up, debug, and optimize software performance, especially in multiprocessing systems. These are software-accessible registers that provide detailed information concerning the dispatch, execution, completion, and memory access of the PowerPC instructions.

Chapter 3. RISC versus CISC

Much debate has been carried out over whether RISC chip architectures are better than CISC architectures. Traditionally, there were features that strongly differentiated RISC architectures from CISC. These features gave each type of architecture particular strengths and weaknesses. This chapter will begin by summarizing the debate and the features that identified each architecture.

Things have been changing very fast since the birth of RISC. Today, if we look at modern CISC and RISC implementations, we will find that they have borrowed many features and techniques from each other. In section 3.3, "RISC and CISC Today" on page 3-4, we will discuss these features that have crossed over from one type of architecture to the other. We will also examine what is left to distinguish CISC and RISC architectures. While doing this, we will emphasize on examples from the latest RISC and CISC implementations such as the PowerPC and the Intel Pentium.

Finally, we will make a comparison between some members of the PowerPC processor family and the Intel Pentium chip.

3.1 Features of RISC and CISC

The following sections describe the features of traditional RISC architectures and contrast them with CISC.

3.1.1 Length and Format of Instructions

A computer program is a very long series of small steps. Each of the steps is called an instruction, represented by a binary number between 1 and 15 bytes long. The binary instruction is loaded from memory into the microprocessor, which decodes and executes it. After execution the instruction is no longer needed and another instruction is loaded into the microprocessor for execution.

Each instruction consists mainly of two parts - the *opcode* and the *operands*. The opcode is the part of the instruction that tells the CPU what operation should be performed. The operands are the data items on which the operation is performed. For example, the operands of an *integer add* operation are two integers, which the CPU adds together with perhaps a third operand telling the CPU where to store the result. The operand of a branch instruction is the target location where the instruction flow jumps to, with perhaps a condition which must be fulfilled for the branch to occur.

In RISC architectures, the instructions are usually of a fixed length, with a simple format. The opcodes are of a fixed length and usually aligned on a word boundary. The simplicity and fixed-length nature of the instructions makes the instruction decoding mechanism much simpler than in a CISC architecture.

CISC architectures usually have variable length instructions. The decoding mechanism in the CPU has to determine the length of the opcode, decode the opcode and then determine the length of the whole instruction and the number of operands following the opcode. This needed more complex instruction decoding mechanisms. More importantly, this meant that the instruction fetch and decoding process took a *variable* number of CPU cycles. The first fetch of an instruction may not bring the whole instruction. The opcode must be decoded before the CPU knows how long the whole instruction is.

CISC architectures have a mix of register-to-register, register-to-memory, and memory-to-memory operations. In some cases, there will be variations of the same operation with these different modes in the same instruction set.

3.1.2 Register-Oriented Operations

RISC architectures use register-to-register operations in most instructions, with only the load and store instructions accessing memory. This is the load/store architecture described in 2.2.2, "Load/Store Architecture" on page 2-11. It is partly the reason why most RISC instructions can execute in one clock cycle. Instructions other than the load and store instructions do not have to handle memory accesses.

3.1.3 Number of Addressing Modes

RISC instructions sets usually contain only a few simple addressing modes. Most of the instructions will use simple register addressing because of the load/store architecture. The only instructions that have to reference memory are the load and store instructions. They usually use no more than two or three simple addressing modes.

In contrast, CISC instruction sets usually contain a larger variety of addressing modes. These addressing modes are used in instructions to access the operands in memory. Typically, the same operation will be implemented in a few instructions, with the different types of addressing modes to access the operands.

3.1.4 Size of Register Sets

RISC architectures usually have many more registers than CISC architectures. While a typical CISC architecture may have eight user-level general-purpose registers, a RISC architecture may have four times that number. In fact, some of the first RISC implementations contained more than 500 registers.

3.1.5 Size of Instruction Sets

The original intent of RISC was to keep the instruction set very small. The first RISC implementations had a set of less than 50 instructions. The instruction set was kept small by removing the complex instructions found in CISC instructions sets. These complex operations were performed in RISC computers by software that emulated a complex instruction with multiple simple instructions.

A small instruction set with simple operations makes it easier to implement all the instructions in hardware. This is called a *hardwired* CPU.

In a CISC technology-based microprocessor, the instruction set consists of hundreds of instructions. A large number of these instructions are not implemented in hardware but broken down into a series of simpler instructions called *microinstructions*. The entire set of microinstructions in a CPU is called *microcode*. Microcode is stored in a functional unit called the *control unit* in the CPU. The control unit takes all the instructions to be executed and translates them to microinstructions, which the CPU then executes. The use of microcode allows the system designer to conserve space on the chip by allowing a large number of instructions to be implemented by combining a far smaller number of microinstructions.

Instructions implemented in microcode create overhead when executed. An instruction would execute faster if hardwired than if translated to microinstructions. But the complexity of many CISC instructions and the state of chip technology at the time RISC was born meant that CISC architectures had to be microcoded.

3.2 Advantages and Disadvantages

The features of traditional RISC and CISC architectures give them certain advantages and disadvantages over each other.

3.2.1 Execution Time

The original motivation for RISC came from studies that showed that a large majority of code in software (about 80%) consists of simple instructions - operations such as add, subtract and assign. Removing the overhead of complex instructions and microcode and implementing the simple instructions in hardware should speed up the execution time of most software.

3.2.2 Pipelining

In 2.2.1, "Pipelining and Superscalar Dispatch" on page 2-7, we saw how implementing pipelining can improve the throughput of the CPU. Pipelining is especially suited to RISC architectures. The fixed-length simple format instructions allow for instruction fetching and decoding in a fixed, regular number of clock cycles. Execution of most instructions can be completed in one cycle because of the simple instructions and hardwired implementation. Because of the simpler, more regular execution process for RISC instructions, pipelining can be more efficiently deployed.

In contrast, imagine implementing pipelining in a CISC CPU. The instruction fetch and decode sequence takes a variable number of clock cycles, depending on the instruction. Some instructions may go through more than one fetch and decode sequence. Memory accesses have to be made to gather the operands for computational instructions. Execution of instructions take a variable number of clock cycles, depending on the number of microinstructions needed to complete the operation.

3.2.3 Optimizing Compilers

Instructions in CISC architectures became more and more complex because the designers were trying to make them look and behave like high-level programming languages. One advantage of having only simple, primitive instructions in RISC architectures was that it would be easier for compilers to optimize code. Compilers perform optimization after compilation. One of the things they do is reorganize the code to try to keep all parts of the processor equally busy. It is easier to reorganize the code if it is made up of simple, primitive instructions than complex instructions that resemble high-level languages.

3.2.4 Code Compatibility

The success of systems based on CISC technology is mainly due to the fact that most applications are compatible on an object code level. The same application can be used across different processor generations. This is because the microcode can be retained from the previous processor with microinstructions added to support the new instructions.

RISC technology provides compatibility not on an object code level but on source code level. Different RISC processors with a different instruction set would require a new compiler.

3.3 RISC and CISC Today

The number of transistors on a single chip in 1980 was limited to only a few thousands. Today, hardware designers can already put between three and four million transistors on a single chip. Because of this advancement in chip technology, today's RISC (PowerPC) and CISC (Pentium)-based processors have more in common than before.

The original intent of reducing the instruction set was to remove the overhead of microcode translation and implement the instructions on hardware to execute faster. The advances in VLSI technology allowed chip designers to implement more complex instructions in hardware. This is the reason why RISC designers can now implement larger and more complex instruction sets without violating the spirit of RISC.

Instructions are what a microprocessor needs to get the work done, and a very high number of instructions directly implemented on a single chip adds immense power to a microprocessor. With today's manufacturing technology there is no longer any need to reduce the instruction set on the microprocessor, as long as there is space available to implement them efficiently.

On the other hand, CISC architectures have also taken advantage of the advances in chip technology to incorporate features that were previously only identified with RISC architectures. For example, the Intel Pentium chip implements simple, single-cycle RISC-style instructions in hardware. These instructions have priority over the microcoded complex instructions during execution. The Pentium also makes heavy use of features such as pipelining, superscalar instruction dispatch, and branch prediction schemes.

Although the two types of architectures have borrowed heavily from each other, there are still some features that can distinguish them:

- The fixed-length nature of RISC instructions versus the variable-length CISC instructions.

  For example, the PowerPC instructions are fixed at 32 bits in length. The Intel x86 instructions vary from 1 to 15 bytes in length.

- Number of addressing modes.

- Size of register sets.

  While the PowerPC has 32 GPRs and 32 FPRs, the Pentium has only 8 GPRs.

3.4 Feature Comparison of CISC and PowerPC Processors

Table 3-1 compares the various features of the PowerPC 601 and 603 chips and the Intel Pentium chip.

Table 3-1 (Page 1 of 3). Comparison Between the PowerPC Processor 601/603 and Pentium			
	PowerPC 601	**PowerPC 603**	**Pentium**
Instruction architecture	RISC	RISC	CISC/RISC

Table 3-1 (Page 2 of 3). Comparison Between the PowerPC Processor 601/603 and Pentium

	PowerPC 601	PowerPC 603	Pentium
Cache	32KB unified	8KB data 8KB instruction	8KB data 8KB instruction
Cache - write policy	Write back or write through	Write back or through (data) Write through (instruction)	Write back or through (data) Write through (instruction)
Cache organization	8-way set associative	2-way set associative (both)	2-way set associative (both)
Cache parity	Parity in cache	No	Parity in Cache
Parity	Parity on all data and address transfers	Parity on all data and address transfers	Parity on all data and address transfers
Superscalar instruction dispatch	3 instructions total per cycle (branch, integer, floating point)	3 instructions total per cycle (branch, integer, floating point)	2 integer per cycle or 2 floating point per cycle
Superscalar execution	3 instructions total per cycle (branch, integer, floating point)	5 instructions total per cycle (each execute unit)	2 integer per cycle or 2 floating point per cycle
Execution units	1 fixed point unit, 1 floating point unit, 1 branch processing unit	1 fixed point unit, 1 floating point unit, 1 branch processing unit, 1 load/store unit, 1 system register unit	2 fixed point units, 1 floating point units
External data bus	64-bit	64-bit	64-bit
External address bus	32-bit	32-bit	32-bit
Word size	32-bit	32-bit	32-bit

	PowerPC 601	**PowerPC 603**	**Pentium**
User registers	32 GPRs, 32 FPRs	32 GPRs, 32 FPRs	8 GPRs, FP stack
Cache line size	64 bytes (two 32-byte sectors)	32 bytes	32 bytes
Out-of-order instruction execution	Yes	Yes	No
Branch prediction	Static	Static	Dynamic
Voltage	3.6 volts	3.3 volts	5.0 volts
Power Consumption	8/9.2 watts; 80MHz, 4 for 100MHz	2/3 watts (80MHz)	13/16 watts (P5); 4/10 watts (P54C)
Number of Transistors	2.8 million	1.6 million	3.1 million
Clock Frequency	50, 66, 80, 100MHz	66, 80MHz	60, 66MHz (P5), 100/66MHz, 90/60MHz (P54C)

3.5 Performance Comparison CISC versus PowerPC

There are several benchmark standards available for evaluating CPUs, but the most widely used standard is the Standard Performance Evaluation Cooperative (SPEC92), a consortium formed by HP, Apollo, MIPS and Sun, to evaluate and compare the performance of CPUs. The consortium designed a set of floating point and integer tests in 1989 that were known as SPEC89 standard. In 1992, these early tests were revised to more accurately reflect the capabilities of newer RISC processors.

SPECint92 and SPECfp92 are benchmark suites that measure integer and floating-point performance of processors.

Figure 3-1 on page 3-9 shows the estimated SPECint92 benchmark figures for integer performance for the Pentium chip and some of the members of the PowerPC family. Figure 3-2 on page 3-10 shows the estimated SPECfp92 figures for floating-point performance. Higher figures mean better performance.

Proper use of the performance estimates is very important. In conjunction with Motorola and Apple, IBM publishes estimated SPECint and SPECfp benchmark results for PowerPC processors when the first silicon milestone is achieved. The SPEC organization allows publishing of reasonable estimated performance results, which are derived from simulation and other techniques. These estimated results are helpful to position the PowerPC processors against rival processors. In combination with other features, such as size and power characteristics, they are useful in indicating the kinds of customers with a preview of the technical capabilities of the PowerPC processor. They do not accurately represent the performance that would be achieved when the PowerPC processor is used in a future system. Actual system performance is dependent on many design characteristics - such as I/O, memory, bus, compilers and cache - that may not be reflected in the SPEC benchmark suite or in simulations. Because of this, actual system performance, especially in low-end, high-volume systems, can be, and often is, lower than estimated performance, especially in low-end, high-volume systems that do not include high performance memory. PowerPC processor performance estimates can not be used in lieu of this to describe future system performance.

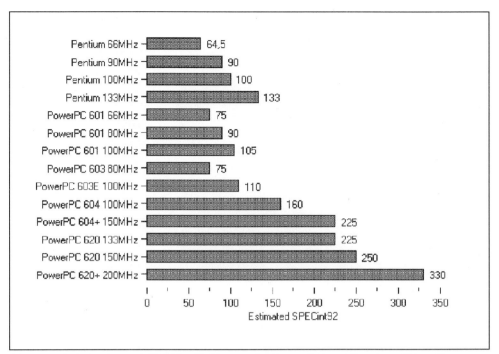

Figure 3-1. *Estimated SPECint92 Figures for PowerPC and Pentium Chips (Source, PowerPC Development Somerset, Austin TX)*

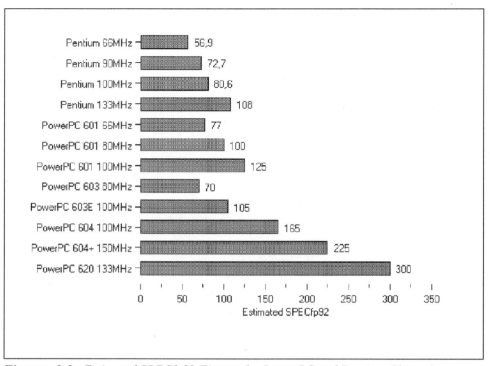

Figure *3-2. Estimated SPECfp92 Figures for PowerPC and Pentium Chips (Source, PowerPC Development Somerset, Austin TX)*

this information, a third party can design a computer that performs the same functions and runs the same system software and applications as a machine produced by Apple, IBM, or Motorola.

The discussion in the rest of this chapter focuses on both the PowerPC Microprocessor Hardware Reference Platform architecture and an initial, or reference, implementation of it currently being developed by Apple, IBM, and Motorola.

An implementation of this architecture must provide for the address maps and register mappings and definitions required by all operating systems that run on that PowerPC Microprocessor Hardware Reference Platform system. It should also support as much common I/O equipment as possible, consistent with cost and size targets for the system.

One of the goals of the developers of the PowerPC Microprocessor Hardware Reference Platform was to minimize the trauma to the various operating systems of having to support new functions from other environments. Several cases had to be considered:

- Unique architectural features: a company had a function unique to its native environment (Power Macintosh or PowerPC Reference Platform). For example, the Apple Desktop Bus (ADB) is unique to the Power Macintosh environment, while the 8042 keyboard interface is used in the PC environment.

- Implementation: a company had its own implementation of a common function, such as audio.

- Growth and evolution: all companies agreed to extend PowerPC Microprocessor Hardware Reference Platform to include new or better functions or implementations of functions.

In the first case, deciding whether to include a function in the PowerPC Microprocessor Hardware Reference Platform architecture was based on whether its function would be useful in the PowerPC Microprocessor Hardware Reference Platform environment. That is, would customers still expect or want it? This was particularly true in the I/O area, where, for example, there are different mouse/keyboard and different serial port architectures between the original PowerPC Reference Platform and Power Macintosh. Also, PowerPC Reference Platform systems support plug-in ISA adapters, which do not exist in the Power Macintosh architecture. To provide broad compatibility, the PowerPC Microprocessor Hardware Reference Platform architecture specifies a minimum set of required functions that supports key features from both environments. In the case of I/O, this means a PowerPC Microprocessor Hardware Reference Platform platform will support I/O from both the Power Macintosh and the original PowerPC Reference Platform environments.

In the second case, factors such as projected market requirements and product cost helped decide which implementation of a function to include in the initial PowerPC Microprocessor Hardware Reference Platform system design. Examples of common functions for which implementation decisions had to be made include the audio subsystem, the storage subsystem (hard disk, floppy, CD-ROM), and the graphics subsystem. The PowerPC Microprocessor Hardware Reference Platform architecture generally does not mandate which particular implementation of a subsystem is required, but it does provide mechanisms to maximize compatibility. For example, IDE or SCSI interfaces are both acceptable for hard disk and CD ROM, and Open Firmware and device drivers will make them compatible in a PowerPC Microprocessor Hardware Reference Platform system. An implementation decision was usually based on the total effort, both hardware and software, required to develop and build a particular implementation. Thus, all other factors being equal, an implementation was chosen to minimize the porting effort of the majority of operating systems that are planned to run on the PowerPC Microprocessor Hardware Reference Platform. That porting effort usually consists of writing new device drivers.

In the third case, architecture decisions will be based on market requirements and industry standards and trends. Implementation decisions will also consider schedule and cost. As technology and market requirements evolve over time, the PowerPC Microprocessor Hardware Reference Platform can change to include these new functions. For example, new infra-red (IR) technology for wireless communication or new serial bus standards can be added to the PowerPC Microprocessor Hardware Reference Platform. Emerging multimedia standards are another example.

It should be noted that the inclusion of the PCI bus architecture in the second-generation Power Macintosh computers was a big step in helping Apple, IBM, and Motorola complete the definition of a common architecture and implementation. The current PowerPC Microprocessor Hardware Reference Platform architecture specifies PCI headers for various functions in an PowerPC Microprocessor Hardware Reference Platform system and could someday be updated to include other bus architectures. The architecture defines how operating systems are informed of the presence of other bus interfaces.

The PowerPC Microprocessor Hardware Reference Platform architecture also specifies the use of the IEEE Standard 1275 for Open Firmware, a technology that makes the computer's hardware configuration process independent of any operating system. The role of Open Firmware in the PowerPC Microprocessor Hardware Reference Platform environment is discussed later in this chapter.

The PowerPC Microprocessor Hardware Reference Platform architecture specification is meant to be an open, industry-standard architecture that will facilitate the rapid growth of PowerPC-based hardware and software.

4.3.4 What the PowerPC Microprocessor Hardware Reference Platform Offers Users

The PowerPC Microprocessor Hardware Reference Platform offers computer users a much more flexible operating environment. They can now buy a computer based on the problems they want to solve, not based on the computer's hardware architecture. The creators of the PowerPC Microprocessor Hardware Reference Platform believe that software, from power-on self-test (POST) and diagnostics to operating systems and applications, drives the usability and acceptance of a computer system. A computer user judges a computer system by its user environment, responsiveness, functionality, and reliability. System software controls these attributes by leveraging the hardware features and performance to provide a total system solution.

All the native operating systems ported to the PowerPC Microprocessor Hardware Reference Platform provide users with their traditional strengths and features. On a single hardware platform a user can now experience superior ease of use and installation of hardware and software, install many industry-standard applications and hardware adapters, and enjoy enhanced networking options.

A customer can buy a PowerPC Microprocessor Hardware Reference Platform and preserve his or her investment in I/O peripherals such as keyboards, displays, printers, telecommunications, etc. As the industry standardizes on PowerPC Microprocessor Hardware Reference Platform, customers will have a wider choice of peripherals and connectivity options. A fundamental goal of the PowerPC Microprocessor Hardware Reference Platform specification is that existing applications that run today on Power Macintosh and PowerPC Reference Platform specification systems will run unchanged on a PowerPC Microprocessor Hardware Reference Platform. Thus, the customer's software investment is also preserved.

4.3.5 Initial PowerPC Microprocessor Hardware Reference Platform Implementation

This section presents a description of the hardware elements in the initial implementation of the PowerPC Microprocessor Hardware Reference Platform. Note that this is only one example of a system design that complies with the PowerPC Microprocessor Hardware Reference Platform architecture. It is not a definition of the architecture, and other implementations may be significantly different. The design of the initial implementation is still under development and can change from that described here.

Detailed information on the initial hardware design will be released by the three companies at a later date. The first customer shipments of compliant hardware are planned to be made in the second half of 1996.

A block diagram of the initial system is shown in Figure 4-5 on page 4-16

4.3.6 Processor

The processor in this system is a PowerPC microprocessor. In this implementation it will be the latest model of the PowerPC 604. It has a 32-bit address bus, providing addressability up to 4 GB. It has a 64-bit data bus.

4.3.7 System Memory (DRAM)

Minimum memory size is 8 MB. Design options are being explored to try to achieve a maximum memory size of 1 GB. 3.3-volt asynchronous DRAMs are planned to be used. The data path is 64 bits with either 8 bits of parity, or ECC, or no protection.

4.3.8 Level 2 (L2) Cache

This implementation supports up to a 1 MB of L2 cache. It has a 64-bit data path with optional 8-bit parity, attached to the processor bus in a "lookaside" configuration. "Lookaside" means that both the L2 cache and the memory controller decode CPU addresses in parallel. The L2 cache can be used in either a write-through or copy-back mode.

Industry-standard cache memory chips will be used. Initial versions of the PowerPC Microprocessor Hardware Reference Platform reference implementation will use asynchronous SRAM. Other versions can use burst SRAM for higher performance. The L2 data and tag SRAMs will be on a card, mounted on a 182-pin ELF connector to simplify upgrades.

The card supports both 5-volt and 3.3-volt components. The motherboard contains 5-volt-tolerant, 3.3-volt buffers for the data SRAM outputs. The tag SRAMs have 3.3-volt drivers. The card will also contain an EEPROM with a serial interface, which will contain presence-detect and other L2 configuration information.

4.3.9 Read-Only Memory (ROM)

The PowerPC Microprocessor Hardware Reference Platform architecture specifies a region for ROM address space. In the initial implementation it is located in the top 16MB of the 4GB address space. The OS ROM is an optional, socketable ROM which is present if the system runs Mac OS. It is 64-bits wide and up to 4MB in size. The system ROM contains boot code, Power-On-Self-Test (POST) code, system Open Firmware code, diagnostics, and other code unique to the hardware configuration in the system. It is 8-bits wide and up to 1MB in size. It is implemented using Flash ROM.

Both ROMs are addressed in the top 16MB of the 4GB address space. The ROMs do not support parity or Error Correction Code (ECC). They are currently 5-volt parts, and the use of 3.3-volt parts is being investigated.

4.3.10 Memory Controller and PCI Bridge

The memory controller and PCI bridge chip in the initial implementation is a follow-on to an existing Motorola part, MCPC105 Eagle. This chip is the interface between the processor bus and the PCI bus and is also the controller for the memory, second level cache (L2), and ROM (processor bus). The processor bus interface is 64 data bits and 32 address bits. The PCI interface is 32 data/address bits. PCI bus speeds of up to 33MHz are supported. The chip uses 3.3 volts. The new functions this ASIC supports for the PowerPC Microprocessor Hardware Reference Platform include:

- A new address map compliant with the PowerPC Microprocessor Hardware Reference Platform architecture. Some legacy address maps from previous architectures may be supported to allow software time to migrate.

- ECC for system memory (DRAM). Controls and checking/generation for a SEC/DED code are provided on the chip.

- ROM controls to handle the two types of ROM present in this implementation.

- Miscellaneous other functional enhancements.

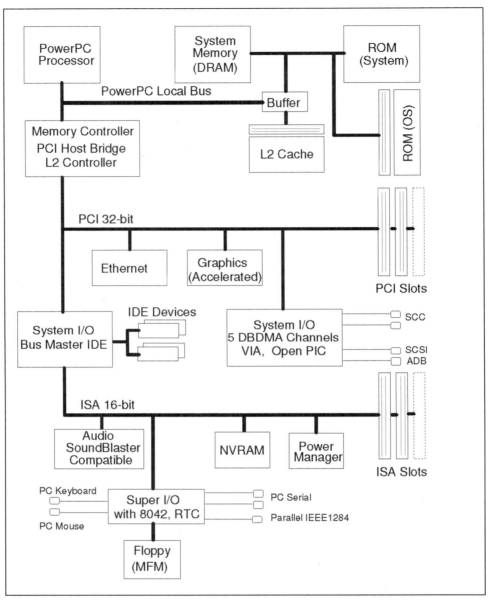

Figure 4-5. *PowerPC Hardware Reference Platform - Initial Implementation Block Diagram*

4.3.11 I/O Subsystem

As discussed previously, an important goal of the PowerPC Microprocessor Hardware Reference Platform is to support I/O peripherals from both the Power Macintosh environment and the PowerPC Reference Platform specification environment. The following section will discuss some of the hardware and software implications of this goal.

4.3.11.1 PCI Devices

The PCI bus is the backbone of the I/O subsystem. There is one PCI bus in the initial implementation. It is compliant with Revision 2.1 of the PCI Standard. The following functions are connected to the PCI bus:

- Graphics subsystem. This implementation has a 64-bit DRAM-based graphics accelerator chip with at least 2 MB of EDO DRAM, which provides high-resolution true color and multimedia capabilities. It has a Bi-Endian frame buffer, controlled by aperture addresses. The chip is a commercially available part and is mounted on the motherboard. In general, a PowerPC Microprocessor Hardware Reference Platform-compliant platform need only ensure that the graphics subsystem support several standard pixel formats and dual-aperture mode for Bi-Endian operations.

- Ethernet. The initial implementation uses a commercially available PCI bus-master Ethernet controller that is mounted on the motherboard.

- Two or three PCI expansion card slots.

- System I/O chip. This chip is mounted on the motherboard and contains general I/O functions. Although the initial implementation supports these functions, not all of them are required by the PowerPC Microprocessor Hardware Reference Platform architecture:

  - Up to 33 MHz PCI bus interface that supports master and slave transactions.

  - PCI Arbiter for six PCI masters plus the CPU.

  - Bus master Enhanced IDE controller. This controller supports two IDE channels (primary and secondary), and supports up to four devices (two per channel). The controller has PCI bus master capability with scatter/gather functions. It also supports PIO modes 0-4 and DMA modes 0- 2. Any operating system that runs on a PowerPC Microprocessor Hardware Reference Platform can boot from the IDE hard drive or CD-ROM. It is also capable of booting from the SCSI hard disk or CD-ROM.

  - PCI/ISA bridge, for 8- and 16-bit ISA devices. This bridge allows ISA mastering by forwarding ISA-master memory references to the PCI bus.

  - Seven-channel DMA between ISA devices and PCI memory, compatible with an 8237 DMA controller. 32-bit DMA addresses are supported.

- 16-channel (cascaded) 8259 interrupt controller function. This controls interrupts from timers and ISA devices. It can be configured with the open programmable interrupt controller (Open PIC) logic on the system I/O-2 chip (see below) so that the combined interrupt structure is compatible with either Intel-based software (for example, Windows) or Mac OS.

- Timer (82C54) functions.

- Miscellaneous decodes and support logic.

- System I/O-2 chip. This chip is mounted on the motherboard and provides the following functions, most of which are related to controlling I/O transfers associated with Mac OS environment. Although the initial implementation supports these functions, not all of them are required by the PowerPC Microprocessor Hardware Reference Platform architecture:

  - Up to 33 MHz PCI bus interface that supports master and slave transactions.

  - Controller for 5 Descriptor-Based DMA (DBDMA) channels. This function performs scatter/gather and process synchronization operations based on control words and a buffer list in main memory.

  - Integrated 85C30 Serial Communications Controller (SCC) cell which supports GeoPort and LocalTalk operations. There are two SCC channels. Each is allocated one DBDMA channel for input and one for output.

  - Apple Desktop Bus (ADB) hardware interface. This is the interface to the Power Macintosh-compatible keyboards, mice, tablets, and other ADB devices.

  - Integrated Versatile Interface Adapter (VIA) cell. In this implementation of the PowerPC Microprocessor Hardware Reference Platform, the VIA cell is used for compatibility with earlier Macintosh interrupt processing.

  - Integrated SCSI-2 controller. One DBDMA channel is allocated.

  - Open programmable interrupt controller (Open PIC) that supports two processors and up to 16 external and I/O interrupts. It can be configured with the 8259 interrupt controller logic on the System I/O chip so that the combined interrupt structure is compatible with either Intel-based (for example, Windows) interrupt-handling software or Mac OS software.

  - Controller for a serial bus used to obtain internal system data for configuration and diagnostics firmware.

4.3.12 ISA Devices

This initial PowerPC Microprocessor Hardware Reference Platform implementation contains an ISA subsystem to maintain compatibility with the many PC style plug-in devices. The bus carries 16 bits of data, 24 bits of addressing, and provides for up to three ISA expansion slots. The System I/O chip described previously is the interface for the ISA subsystem to the PCI bus. The functions in the initial implementation provide the following services, which are either required or supported by the PowerPC Microprocessor Hardware Reference Platform architecture:

- Audio Subsystem. SoundBlaster compatibility is provided by a commercially available chip mounted on the motherboard. The system provides separate DMA channels for stereo recording and playback.

- Power Management Chip. This chip is mounted on the motherboard and provides hardware control and interfaces to support the various system power-managed states, including hibernate and Mac OS SoftPower function. The chip is a microcontroller that responds to activities such as modem rings and mouse or keyboard signals. It provides power management interrupts and power supply control. The controller is powered by a separate 5 V auxiliary power supply which is powered on whenever AC is applied.

- Super I/O Chip. In the initial implementation, this chip provides interfaces for:
  - Floppy Disk interface equivalent to the NS82077 controller. Auto-sense and auto-eject are supported for 1.44 MB (formatted) MFM drives. GCR disk format is not supported by the PowerPC Microprocessor Hardware Reference Platform architecture nor by this implementation. One ISA DMA channel is allocated for the floppy device.
  - Parallel Port. IEEE 1284 EPP and ECP are supported. One ISA DMA channel is allocated for the parallel port.
  - Two serial ports, software-compatible with PC16550. The controller decodes COM ports 1-4.
  - PC-compatible keyboard and mouse control is provided by Intel 8042-compliant logic.
  - Real Time Clock (RTC) PC-compatible functions.
  - Infra-red controller (IrDA, HP).

- NVRAM, implemented as an 8K x 8 discrete chip.

- Three ISA slots.

4.3.13 Open Firmware

The PowerPC Microprocessor Hardware Reference Platform architecture requires all compliant systems to implement the Open Firmware startup process defined by IEEE 1275-1994 Standard for Boot (Initialization, Configuration) Firmware, and the PCI Binding to IEEE 1275-1994 specification. These standards evolved from the OpenBoot firmware architecture introduced by Sun Microsystems. The Open Firmware startup process is driven by startup firmware, also called boot firmware, in system ROM and in ROM chips on expansion cards. While the startup firmware is running, the computer will power up and configure its hardware (including peripheral devices) independently of any operating system. The computer will then find an operating system on a mass storage device or in ROM, load it into system memory, and terminate the Open Firmware startup process by giving that operating system control of the PowerPC processor. The six native operating systems mentioned earlier are planned to run on a PowerPC Microprocessor Hardware Reference Platform-compliant system with Open Firmware.

The startup firmware includes these specific features:

It is written in the Forth language, as defined by IEEE Standard 1275. Firmware code is stored in an abbreviated representation called FCode. The computer's startup firmware includes a loader and interpreter that will install FCode in system memory. Firmware in expansion card ROMs can modify the Open Firmware startup process by supplying device-specific FCode that the computer's firmware loads and runs before launching an operating system.

- The startup process creates a data structure of nodes called a device tree, in which the characteristics of the hardware system and of each peripheral device are described by property lists. The device tree is stored in system memory. The operating system that is ultimately installed and launched will search the device tree to determine the nature and characteristics of available hardware. The device tree can also store runtime drivers, written in the PowerPC instruction set, for various combinations of devices and operating systems.

- System firmware includes a basic set of device drivers and associated resources such as fonts, written in FCode, that are required during system startup before an operating system is running. Plug-in expansion cards that are used during startup may also contain driver code. The firmware in system ROM installs these drivers in system memory so they can be executed on the PowerPC processor.

- Firmware in system ROM may also contain debugging facilities for both FCode and some kinds of operating system code.

4.3.14 Summary

The PowerPC Microprocessor Hardware Reference Platform will effectively bring together the two worlds of PowerPC-based systems, namely the PowerPC Reference Platform specification-compliant systems and the Apple Power Mac-compliant systems. PowerPC Microprocessor Hardware Reference Platform will replace the PowerPC Reference Platform specification and ultimately define an open standard for PowerPC processor-based personal computers.

Chapter 5. PowerPC Software Environment

Technology, as everyone knows, is advancing rapidly. Microprocessors are getting faster and faster, actually doubling the performance every 14 to 18 months. Additionally, every new generation of microprocessors is offered at a better price/performance ratio. In the area of communications, bandwidths are increasing to the point where handling multimedia data streams becomes practical.

Mobile and wireless communications are gaining presence in the market, and interactive TV and the information highway are not far behind. The digitization of data is changing the way we manage information. CD-ROM technology is improving the storage capabilities and decreasing the cost of information distribution. Mixing data types of speech, pen and video in the same document or the same application is now feasible.

As the technology and the power of personal systems have increased, so has the complexity of developing operating systems and applications. This complexity has created a new set of issues and challenges, in particular for independent software developers (ISVs), and for end users. In Chapter 4, "PowerPC Strategy" on page 4-1 we discussed the PowerPC strategy - a strategy that will provide an open environment and simplify the development of new operating systems and applications. This chapter provides an overview of PowerPC operating systems and application development tools.

5.1 Operating Systems for PowerPC

IBM is creating an *open* standard. The microprocessors are from a collaboration between IBM, Apple and Motorola. The PowerPC Reference Platform specification is open to all manufacturers. The option cards fit in industry-standard open buses, and systems are designed to run a wide range of operating systems.

The goal is to support a wide range of applications. Applications written for the major 32-bit operating systems, such as OS/2, UNIX and Windows NT are supported natively. Available 16-bit applications (for example, DOS and Windows applications) are supported via various compatibility techniques on these 32-bit operating systems.

The initial operating systems being ported to the PowerPC Reference Platform specification include OS/2 Warp Connect (PowerPC Edition), AIX, Windows NT, and Solaris.

5.1.1 IBM OS/2 Warp Connect (PowerPC Edition)

The strategic operating system for the IBM Personal Computer Power Series and the IBM ThinkPad Power Series product line is OS/2 Warp Connect (PowerPC Edition).

OS/2 Warp Connect (PowerPC Edition) will continue the OS/2 tradition of providing the most flexible, integrated, reliable and usable client environment for personal productivity applications. The IBM Power Series will provide the best price/performance platforms in the industry for these applications. Wordprocessing, spreadsheets, electronic mail, office functions, and many other productivity applications will be supported, as will leading-edge implementations of multimedia. OS/2 Warp Connect (PowerPC Edition) will also provide a powerful environment for interactive education and training applications at all levels, and will be a superior high-end platform for the home computing environment.

In combination with products such as LAN Server, Communication Manager/2, DB2/2, CICS/2, IMS/2, and TCP/IP, OS/2 Warp Connect (PowerPC Edition) will also function as a server for file and device sharing, database transactions, application sharing and gateways.

OS/2 Warp Connect (PowerPC Edition) will operate as a full-function, high-performance client system, running 16-bit DOS and DOS/Windows applications, as well as 16-bit and 32-bit OS/2 applications. OS/2 32-bit applications will run natively after being recompiled using a cross-compiler. Applications with 16-bit calls will employ a conversion tool that identifies the 16-bit calls and, optionally, converts them to 32-bit.

5.1.1.1 Endian Mode and Multiprocessing

OS/2 Warp Connect (PowerPC Edition) runs in Little-Endian mode and is currently not multiprocessing enabled.

5.1.1.2 Application Base

Applications for OS/2 Warp Connect (PowerPC Edition) are written at several levels:

- OS/2 32-bit PowerPC native applications

- DOS and Windows 16-bit Intel emulation applications

32-bit applications written for Intel X86 versions of OS/2 are source-level compatible with the OS/2 Warp Connect (PowerPC Edition). Such applications can make full use of the machine's graphics capabilities using Presentation Manager.

Existing Intel X86-architecture DOS and DOS/Windows-based applications can be run in DOS mode using an instruction set emulator (ISE). Emulation capabilities are available for 80486 ring 3, DOS 6.3, Windows 3.11, and WIN32s. OS/2 Warp Connect (PowerPC Edition) also provides a full emulation of both DOS and Windows.

OS/2 Warp Connect (PowerPC Edition) supports the FAT (DOS), HPFS, and ISO 9660 file systems.

5.1.1.3 Microkernel Strategy and OS/2

IBM's intention is to create operating systems independent of any specific hardware platform, so that any operating system can run on any hardware architecture. The hardware independence will lead to operating systems that are portable between different hardware architectures.

The operating system consists of software components and application frameworks. These are modular and designed to be taken apart and put back together in different combinations across different platforms.

Following are the different components:

- IBM Microkernel

  The IBM Microkernel is based on the Mach 3.0 Microkernel developed at the Carnegie Mellon University. The IBM Microkernel is the basic building block from which operating systems can be built.

- Operating System Personalities

  Personalities are environments that run given sets of applications on top of the IBM Microkernel. The *personality* contains the elements that users recognize as a particular operating system today. This includes the look and feel of the system (user interface) and the ability to run a specific set of applications (programming interface). Multiple operating system personalities can co-exist on the IBM Microkernel. For example, there could be an operating system personality that runs OS/2 applications, another one that runs DOS/Windows applications. Other operating system personalities can be added in a modular way.

- Shared Services

  Each shared service provides functions that are not bound to a particular personality but may be required by an application running in any personality. Thus they can be provided for use by multiple personalities. Examples of functions that could be provided as shared services are:

  - Device drivers

  - Default paging mechanism

  - File access

  - Multimedia support

  - Network communications

  - Database engine

Several of these services are shipped along with the IBM Microkernel. Additional services are optional and can be added and deleted as deemed necessary by the user.

The *personality* could of course provide these functions itself, but by delegating these tasks to other shared services, dedicated to those functions, will result in a number of important advantages.

- The dedicated shared services can be used by multiple personalities.

- The dedicated shared services can be independently maintained and upgraded.

- The complexity of the personality is reduced.

An example of the shared services is the file system. This service provides the core functions of opening, closing, reading from and writing to files. This service is provided to all personalities. This significantly simplifies the OS/2 or DOS file support. From an application point of view, the existence of these services are hidden by the personality's application programming interface.

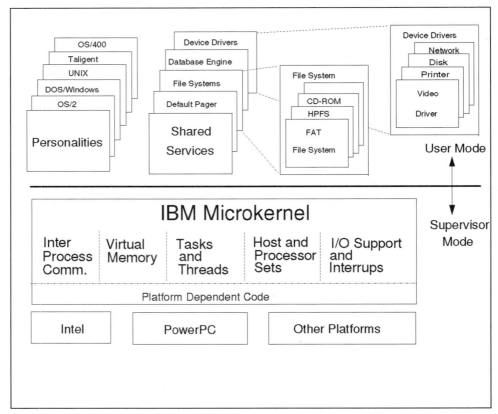

Figure 5-1. *The Microkernel Architecture*

Figure 5-1 shows the structure of an IBM Microkernel-based operating system. The underlying hardware is managed by the IBM Microkernel. All the other components are user-level processes (shared services) such as device drivers, file system, default pager, and the operating system personalities. Applications are written to the interfaces provided by the personality. This structure allows to easily support multiple hardware platforms while ensuring portability of the operating system and user applications.

5.1.1.4 Hardware Abstraction Layer - IBM Microkernel

The IBM Microkernel-based technology enables the operating system to be independent of the type of hardware architecture. This is accomplished by rearranging the functions of the traditional operating system into simplified modular building blocks. The most essential functions of the operating system are contained in the *Microkernel* module, and only a small part of that module is hardware-dependent. Other operating system services are contained in separate modules and are *not* hardware-platform dependent.

5.1.1.5 Device Driver Model

Traditionally, device drivers are loaded into the kernel at boot time and then run as part of the kernel at supervisor level. Since the device drivers act as kernel extensions, they are not portable to other operating systems and other hardware platforms. This requires a new device driver for each operating system. Furthermore a software failure in a device driver has the same catastrophic effect as a software failure in the kernel. This has significant implications for the robustness of the system.

In the Workplace OS architecture, device drivers are provided as common services running at user-level. In other words, device drivers are shared across all the personalities and their applications.

User-level device drivers gain access to devices using IBM Microkernel functions which grant them rights to specific memory resources. A small piece of the device driver is injected into the IBM Microkernel as an interrupt handler. The interrupt handler has a very restricted set of functions it can perform.

By isolating the drivers into independent tasks, they can be developed and debugged using standard development tools. They have access to the full function set, and are no longer in a position to corrupt the kernel with a bug in driver code. This is a significant enhancement to the integrity of the system. Making user-level device drivers into normal tasks also makes it easier to add and delete device drivers without re-booting the system.

A device driver development kit is available from IBM. It contains all the documentation and sample code needed to develop device drivers. In addition, DOS device drivers may be used to access devices from a virtual DOS session.

5.1.2 IBM AIX

AIX, the IBM version of the UNIX operating system, is a scalable, robust and reliable operating system designed to meet stringent system requirements while also implementing all prevalent open systems standards. Perhaps the most important aspect of AIX is that it is offered on the widest range of systems in the industry. It provides a common operating environment look-and-feel, a common programming environment, and a single application binary interface across a broad range of computing power from notebooks to teraflop systems.

Since AIX is such a high-capacity operating system, it normally appears on systems that can support extremely large amounts of data and very high rates of computation. Additionally, it has significant communications capabilities as it supports - in addition to TCP/IP - the SNA and OSI protocol and it is an integral part of IBM's Network Blueprint and Open Blueprint.

The market acceptance of UNIX on workstations has not been as widespread as the personal computer operating systems such as DOS/Windows and OS/2. This was mainly due to two reasons:

- UNIX required relatively more investment in hardware.

- The traditional user interface was considered too difficult to learn for general users to accept.

These barriers are disappearing because of recent developments:

- New low-cost processors will make it possible to develop UNIX workstations that are more affordable. For example, IBM will offer AIX on the IBM Power Series family. This range of machines will be very cost-effective as personal UNIX workstations.

- Graphical-user interfaces such as COSE desktop are now standard components of popular versions of UNIX, such as AIX. This greatly increases the ease of use of UNIX.

5.1.2.1 Endian Mode and Multiprocessing

AIX runs in Big-Endian mode and is designed to support symmetric multiprocessing (SMP) with no limit on the number of processors supported.

5.1.2.2 Hardware Abstraction Layer

The AIX kernel has a modular structure and a formalized and well-documented set of interfaces. These attributes will persist across operating system releases and can achieve many of the same goals as the abstraction software.

The routines in the kernel that interfaces to hardware components are provided by a set of services to perform a requested function independent of the underlying hardware platform.

The main components of the AIX kernel fall into the categories of services that account for differences in the processor, I/O, and platform-specific implementations. Typical services provided under this framework are memory management services (cache and DMA), access to bus controllers and system I/O (I/O services), boot/configuration services (hardware initialization), interrupts, device drivers and RAS (access to NVRAM and system error registers).

The kernel hardware services make the underlying hardware accessible to the kernel, device drivers, and subsystems in an abstract manner. The service invoked by the routines within the system components remains the same for any hardware platform.

5.1.2.3 Device Driver Model

Device drivers run in a privileged state as AIX kernel extensions, and have access to a number of functions that are unavailable to normal application programs. They shield the user from device-specific details and provide a common I/O model for accessing the devices for which they provide support.

Device drivers can play two roles in AIX: the *device head* role and the *device handler* role.

A device head is a device driver or a portion of a device driver that provides an interface to application programs via the standard *open, close, read, write,* and related system calls. A device driver acting in this role takes I/O requests from application programs and communicates them to a device handler. The interface between application programs and a device head is rigidly defined by the AIX kernel itself.

A device handler is the portion of a device driver that communicates with the actual device or adapter. The device handler takes requests from a device head and implements the request on real hardware. The interface between a device head and a device handler is essentially undefined by AIX, though a large number of primitive functions are provided by AIX to assist in constructing the interface. The details are left to the device driver author. The interface between the device handler and device itself is naturally dependent on the hardware being manipulated, though AIX again provides a set of functions which assist in performing the hardware interface.

Most simple device drivers will in fact act as both device head and device handler, but other configurations are possible. Vendors who offer a system with components different from those in the reference implementation must support this differentiation with a device driver.

5.1.2.4 Application Base

Powerful emulation services are provided for users who want to move to AIX while still
having the opportunity to use their current applications and computer knowledge. The
benefit of this approach is that users have a choice between different environments
(DOS, Windows, Macintosh, or UNIX) as well as the multitude of applications that exist
within those environments. Figure 5-2 conceptually shows the emulation strategy of
AIX. WabiPlus and MAS will be covered in 5.2, "PowerPC Application Support" on
page 5-14.

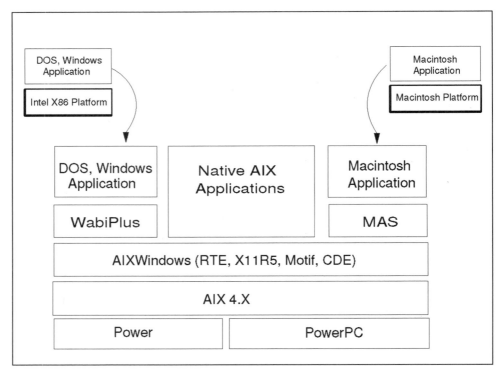

Figure   *5-2. DOS/Windows and Macintosh Applications on AIX*

5.1.3 Microsoft Windows NT

Windows NT is a full, 32-bit, preemptive multitasking operating system. It will run
existing MS-DOS and Windows applications as well as new 32-bit applications being
developed by independent software vendors on the PowerPC Reference Platform
specification. It is capable of fully utilizing the advanced capabilities of the PowerPC
microprocessors, from today's 601/603 versions to those of the future.

Windows NT and the IBM Power Series will provide the reliability required by information systems professionals and power users to run demanding business applications. The advanced microkernel design of Windows NT, combined with integrated security, manageability and quality of the IBM Power Series, will meet the needs of corporations deploying business critical applications.

Windows NT is designed to be a portable operating system capable of running on all popular microprocessor architectures. This provides the ability to deploy Windows NT/IBM Power Series solutions that integrate fully and have the same user interface as other systems in the enterprise. This results in lower training investment while also protecting customer investment of existing systems and applications until they are supplemented with newer and more powerful solutions.

5.1.3.1 Endian Mode and Multiprocessing
Windows NT runs in Little-Endian mode and is capable of supporting up to two microprocessors in SMP mode.

5.1.3.2 Operating System Configuration
Windows NT is a multi-user system which operates either as stand-alone or as a client in a network. Windows NT Workstation is a full implementation including the base operating system, file systems, and the C2 security features. It can also act as a file/print resource on a network.

Several utilities are included such as performance/event monitoring, backup, remote access, network client support, disk maintenance and a user configuration/account profile utility. In addition, the product includes electronic mail and personal/workgroup scheduling applications. The Windows NT Workstation version is capable of supporting up to two microprocessors in SMP mode.

5.1.3.3 Hardware Abstraction Layer
This layer resides between the NT executive and the hardware platform on which Windows NT is running. It hides hardware-dependent details such as I/O interfaces, interrupt controllers, and multiprocessor communication mechanisms from the rest of the operating system.

5.1.3.4 Device Driver Model
There is a separate Device Driver Development Kit (DDK) available from both Microsoft and Motorola. It contains all the documentation and sample code needed to develop device drivers.

5.1.3.5 Application Base
Windows NT supports native applications conforming to Microsoft's 32-bit Windows API.

At a source level, the APIs provided by NT are identical across all architectures supported by NT (MIPS, Alpha, X86, PowerPC). Applications written to these APIs are independent of the underlying hardware, and require only recompilation to generate executable code that will run on Windows NT across all supported architectures.

At a binary level, applications built to run on Windows NT will run unchanged across all PowerPC platforms supported by NT.

In addition to Win32 applications, Windows NT runs existing DOS and 16-bit Windows applications as well as some 16-bit OS/2 text applications and all POSIX-conforming (IEEE1003.1) applications.

5.1.4 Sunsoft Solaris

Solaris is a 32-bit UNIX operating system, owned and marketed by SunSoft, Inc., a software division of Sun Microsystems Computer Corporation (SMCC). As a fully compliant implementation of Systems V Release 4 UNIX (SVR4), Solaris provides access to the most powerful and advanced solutions available, including an open, networked environment. Solaris also unites the world's largest installed base of CISC and RISC hardware, SPARC, Intel X86, and PowerPC.

The SunOS 5.x operating system is the foundation of Solaris. The innovative technology it contains - including the industry's leading implementation of a multithreading operating system - brings a new level of performance to Solaris users. SunOS 5.x builds on SVR4 and extends it by introducing new features, including symmetric multiprocessing with a multithreaded kernel, real-time functionality, advanced internationalization, and increased security features.

Solaris features OpenWindows, SunSoft's X11 network-based windows system. With its windows, pull-down menus, buttons and drag-and-drop operations, OpenWindows provides a consistent easy-to-use environment for all types of users. The DeskSet desktop productivity tools feature integrated distributed tools, from basic time-management applications through sophisticated workgroup communications tools. SunSoft's ToolTalk interapplication communication solution facilitates information exchange between applications on a single machine, or on multiple machines on a network.

Large companies looking to right size their operations will find Solaris is a good solution for supporting heterogeneous hardware environments, ranging from notebooks to high-end multiprocessor servers using X86, SPARC and PowerPC architectures.

5.1.4.1 Endian Mode and Multiprocessing

Solaris runs on the PowerPC Reference Platform specification in Little-Endian mode and is designed to support symmetric multiprocessing with no fixed limit to the number of processors. Platform-specific modules may need to be written to support a particular multiprocessing platform. Specifications for writing such modules are available from SunSoft.

5.1.4.2 Operating System Configuration

Solaris is offered in the following three configurations:

- Desktop

  This configuration is targeted at end users and desktop developers for use as clients on a network or as stand-alone workstations.

- Workgroup Server

  This configuration is targeted at departmental servers for use as print, file, database, or application servers on a small network with up to 100 users. The license allows unlimited use but is restricted to platforms with a maximum of two CPUs.

- Enterprise Server

  This configuration supports high-end multiprocessor servers. There is no limit to the number of processors, but the configuration is targeted primarily at MPs with no more than 20 processors. It supplements the basic Solaris functionality with additional components for disk management (RAID), network backup, and advanced network system administration.

5.1.4.3 Hardware Abstraction Layer

The Solaris kernel can be dynamically tailored by means of platform-independent modules (PIMs), which provide a common support for all platforms on a processor architecture that implements a particular feature. For example, a loadable module might support a particular device or controller, a particular bus (for example PCI), a particular file system format such as ISO 9660, a particular scheduling class or a particular networking protocol. Such loadable modules are usually generated from source code that is common across all processor architectures.

Platform-specific modules (PSMs), on the other hand, support functions whose implementation differs from one platform to another. The kernel binary interface (KBI) spells out the interface to which independent hardware providers code platform support modules. The KBI is an extension and formalization of the technology that has been successfully employed for multiprocessor platform support on both SPARC and X86.

A generic distribution of Solaris from Sunsoft supports one or more base system configurations. It contains a kernel, a set of device and bus interface modules, a complete UNIX System V Release 4 environment, Solaris Deskset tools, system administration software, and subroutine libraries.

5.1.4.4 Device Driver Model

The Solaris Device Driver Interface (DDI) provides a well-documented and stable base for device driver development. The DDI consists of a common base interface with minor extensions for each of the various processor architectures. Most drivers written for devices that work under Solaris on X86 can be recompiled without source change and run on PowerPC systems. The DDI is supported by a Driver Development Kit (DDK), which consists of descriptions and technical documentation of the interfaces as well as sample drivers.

5.1.4.5 Application Base

Solaris supports native applications conforming to the System V Interface Definition (SVID), the generic System V Application Binary Interface (gABI), and the PowerPC processor supplement to the System V ABI (PowerPC psABI).

At a source level, the APIs provided by Solaris are identical across all architectures supported by Solaris (SPARC, X86, PowerPC). Applications written to these APIs are independent of the underlying hardware, and require only recompilation to generate binaries that will run on Solaris across all supported architectures.

At a binary level, applications built to run on Solaris/PowerPC will run unchanged across all PowerPC platforms supported by Solaris.

Emulation programs which are not part of the operating system are expected to be available to run applications from other environments, such as Windows, DOS, or Macintosh.

Solaris supports the executable and link format (ELF) object module format as defined in the SVR4 PowerPC ABI.

Solaris can import non-native file systems such as High Sierra (ISO 9660), FAT (DOS), and S5 (UNIX System V).

5.1.5 PowerPC Operating Systems Comparison

The following table provides a comparison between the different operating systems for the PowerPC Personal System based systems:

Table 5-1. *Operating System Comparison*

	OS/2 Warp Connect (PowerPC Edition)	AIX	Windows NT	Solaris	System 7
PowerPC Reference Platform specification	Yes	Yes	Yes	Yes	No
RS/6000	No	Yes	No	No	No
PowerMac	No	No	No	No	Yes
Endian mode	Little	Big	Little	Little	Big
GUI	Workplace Shell	CDE AIXWindows	Program Manager	CDE/Motif	Finder
Multi Processing Model	no	SMP	SMP	SMP	no
Multi-tasking Model	Preemptive	Preemptive	Preemptive	Preemptive	Cooperative
No. of CPUs supported	N/A	unlimited	2/4	unlimited	N/A
DOS/Win16 Applications Support	MVM Server	WabiPlus SoftWindows	SoftWindows	Wabi or WabiPlus SoftWindows	SoftWindows
680x0 Mac Application Support	No	Yes (MAS)	No	Yes (MAS)	Yes
Vendor	IBM	IBM	Microsoft	SunSoft	Apple

5.1.6 Apple System 7

IBM was the first computer company offering workstations based on PowerPC technology, while Apple introduced the first personal computer systems using this technology. The Power Macintosh systems ship with System 7, which can be summarized as follows:

- Version 7.1.2 of System 7 can make some native calls to the PowerPC. Subsequent releases of System 7 will take more advantage of native calls to the PowerPC processors.

- A ROM-based emulation chip (called the 68LC040) is installed to support running the existing 680X0-based software without recompiling.

- In order to support 16-bit DOS and Windows applications, System 7 contains emulation products from Insignia, SoftWindows.

- Power Macintosh is not PowerPC Reference Platform specification compliant. It comes with Apple's proprietary NuBus expansion slot.

Figure 5-3 shows the System 7 on the Power Macintosh. System 7 for PowerPC relies on built-in emulation not only for compatibility with 680X0-based Mac applications, but also for its own Toolbox routines that are not ported yet.

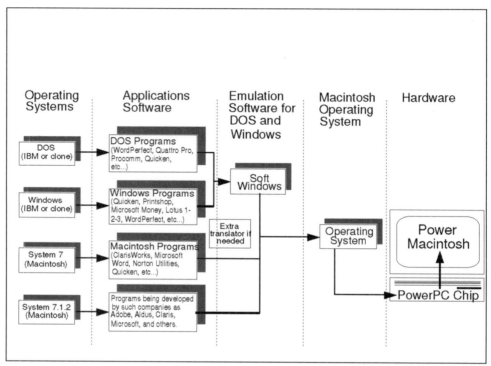

Figure *5-3.* *The Apple System 7 on the Power Macintosh*

5.2 PowerPC Application Support

Supporting many operating systems creates the ability to run an exceptionally wide range of applications, spanning both the personal computer and workstation worlds. On the PowerPC platform, applications written for the major 32-bit operating systems, such as UNIX, OS/2 and Windows NT can be supported natively. 16-bit applications, such as

DOS, Windows and Macintosh, will be supported via various compatibility techniques on these 32-bit systems.

- DOS applications will be supported on OS/2 Warp Connect (PowerPC Edition) through the same type of multiple virtual DOS machines as on OS/2. On AIX, DOS applications are supported via WabiPlus and SoftWindows. Windows NT support for DOS applications on the IBM Power Series is the same as for any other version of NT.

- Windows applications will be supported on OS/2 Warp Connect (PowerPC Edition) as they are currently supported under OS/2 2.1. Both AIX and Solaris employ Wabi SoftWindows, the Windows application binary interface. Windows NT support for Windows applications is the same as for all other versions of NT.

- Macintosh applications will be supported on AIX using a Macintosh emulator called Macintosh Application Support (MAS).

- OS/2 16-bit applications will need to be converted to 32-bit and recompiled. OS/2 32-bit applications can run natively after being recompiled using a cross-compiler. For applications with 16-bit calls, a conversion tool will be made available that identifies the 16-bit calls and optionally converts them to 32-bit.

Performance is always an important item. The best performance will, of course, be achieved by native applications that fully exploit the PowerPC's inherent RISC performance advantages. These includes existing AIX applications as well as OS/2, Solaris and NT applications recompiled or newly developed for the PowerPC Reference Platform specification.

Wabi employs a mixture of native execution and emulation technologies for Windows applications running on AIX and Solaris. Most portions of these Windows programs will benefit from the so-called *Wabi Effect*, that is, native RISC-level performance

Macintosh and DOS applications on UNIX, as well as DOS and Windows applications on OS/2 Warp Connect (PowerPC Edition), will initially run at PC speeds. The individual operating systems vendors are hard at work to further improve the performance of the various compatibility technologies.

In addition to the operating systems vendors who have already announced support, IBM is working with producers of other 32-bit operating systems, and there is interest on the part of a number of them to announce support for the PowerPC Reference Platform specification.

Likewise, an increasing number of independent software vendors are planning to recompile or otherwise port their applications to run natively on the Platform. This number will continue to grow. Exciting new applications from ISVs and from IBM will take advantage of such innovations as embedded multimedia devices, higher bandwidth networks, and higher resolution graphics.

The IBM Power Series will provide strong support for existing 16-bit applications as well as a platform of growth for the personal computer and workstations of the future. Software and application support plays a critical role in the future success of the PowerPC. It is the single most important factor ensuring the success of IBM's new endeavor in the field of personal desktop computing.

5.2.1 PowerPC Application Compatibility and Porting

Compatibility with existing application products is a key factor for acceptance of new technology. The market would not accept new technology if the users could not run their favorite software, or had to spend additional money for a new license. Software compatibility is a complicated subject. Generally speaking, application compatibility refers to an operating system's ability to execute application programs written for other operating systems or for earlier versions of the same operating systems.

There are actually two levels of compatibility:

- *Binary Compatibility*

  This is achieved when an executable program (binary code) can be run on a different operating system.

- *Source-level compatibility*

  This level requires recompiling programs before running them on the new system.

Binary compatibility is not easy between processors based on different architectures. Compatibility in this situation is normally provided by using software emulation programs. Without an emulator, all applications must be recompiled (see source-level compatible), or rewritten.

To run software on different platforms, be it a different processor architecture or a different operating system, requires changes.

There are four methods of porting an application:

- *Manual Re-coding*

  Rewriting platform-dependent portions of a program is the surest way to future maintainability. Compiler optimization from original, intelligently structured sources assure superior performance. However, the effort required to manually re-code programs depends upon the portability of the source language and the degree of modularity.

- *Automated Source Translation*

Employing a source-level translation tool may assist in the manual re-coding of large projects. Their use should be limited to smaller *straightforward* modules. If exercised on complex code, manual intervention may be necessary, and generated results are normally cryptic.

- *Static Binary Translation*

  Static optimizations tend to be more thorough and elaborate than what is possible by run-time emulation. The translation effort is greater and may need human management. Resultant binaries are not maintainable.

- *Binary Emulation*

  Products such as Wabi or SoftWindows and operating systems such as OS/2 and Windows NT attempt to mimic the program's original operating environment as well as translate instructions "on-the-fly". Little or no human intervention is necessary, since both the program's platform and code are being emulated. However, performance penalties for dynamic translation have to be considered.

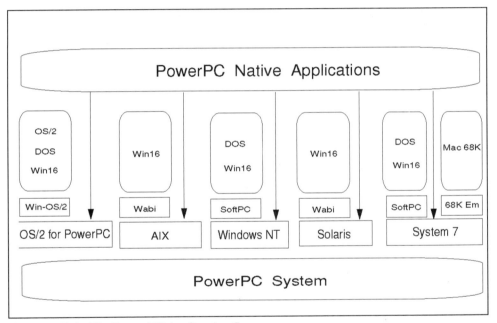

Figure 5-4. *The PowerPC Application Support*

Since the majority of desktop applications are written for DOS and Windows, several emulation solutions are available from various vendors to run these 16-bit applications on the new 32-bit PowerPC operating systems:

- DOS, Windows on OS/2 Warp Connect (PowerPC Edition)

The multiple virtual machine (MVM) environment is part of the OS/2 Warp Connect (PowerPC Edition) and responsible for providing DOS/Windows/DPMI program compatibility. OS/2 Warp Connect (PowerPC Edition) provides DOS 6.3 and Windows 3.1 compatibility on a PowerPC. OS/2 provides an almost perfect environment for DOS and Windows applications on the PowerPC platform. This is done in the following way:

- Boot a DOS emulation kernel in a virtual machine.

- Boot raw DOS (DR-DOS, DOS V3.3 and above) in a virtual machine.

- Run multiple DOS applications concurrently in the system.

- Run DOS applications full screen or windowed.

- Provides LIM EMS 4.0, LIMA XMS 2.0, and DPMI 1.0 host support.

- Provides support for Windows 3.0 and 3.1 applications by running WIN-OS/2.

- Provides support for network redirection of drives in a virtual machine or a DOS application.

- Provides user configuration support for the MVM environment on a per virtual machine basis.

- Support for Win32 applications may be added as the marketplace matures.

  IBM's Instruction Set Translator (IST) technology is used here. The IST translates Intel instructions on non-Intel machines, such as the PowerPC. It provides 486 ring 3 protected-mode and real-mode instructions. The IST is the only module that understands Intel instructions, and provides services that the rest of MVM depend on to run DOS and Windows applications on a PowerPC.

• DOS, Windows on UNIX

Insignia Solutions' SoftWindows or IBM/Sunselect's WabiPlus are the emulation choices for UNIX on the PowerPC (AIX and Solaris). Both support the installation and execution of shrink-wrapped Windows 3.1 applications under UNIX, and operate as separate UNIX processes.

- SoftWindows, a re-engineered and recompiled version of SoftPC 3.1, is essentially a source-code port of Microsoft Windows with a proprietary 286-level emulator. It is a very good emulation of MS Windows, but performance suffers somewhat, since some Windows internals are emulated. Another consideration is its memory requirement. SoftWindows requires at least 9MB of memory to operate, and 12MB to support Windows multitasking at a reasonable speed.

- Wabi provides API-level compatibility with Windows and relies on a portable emulation engine. This engine will be replaced with IBM's Instruction Set Translator in WabiPlus. Since Wabi does not duplicate the internal structure of

Windows, it tends to perform better than SoftWindows for graphics-oriented programs. However, certain undocumented API nuances and behaviors are not emulated, which prevent some ill-behaved applications from running atop of Wabi. WabiPlus, an enhanced version of Wabi, has additional features:

- IBM's high performance IST (instruction set translator)

- DOS and DOS application support

  - IBM's PCHE (PC hardware environment)

    - VGA and SVGA (256 color VESA standard)

    - Keyboard, disk and diskette controller

    - Timer, speaker, serial and parallel ports

    - Virtual 86 with DPMI, LIM, and XMS

  - PC DOS 6.x and MS DOS 6.x support

  - Common configuration of DOS and Windows environment

- DOS, Windows on System 7

Insignia Solutions' SoftWindows is also available on the Power Macintosh.

5.2.2 PowerPC Application Development Tools and Support

This section provides details on the available development tools and established support organizations for software developers who want to develop or port applications to the PowerPC platform.

5.2.2.1 PowerPC Application Development Tools

PowerPC Compiler: A compiler translates source code written in a high level languages such as C, C++, Fortran, or Pascal into executable object code. Object code is often subsequently linked to other objects or support libraries before being loaded into memory.

A *cross* compiler differs from a *native* compiler in that the compiler itself runs on a different platform than that of the target object. For example, a PowerMac cross compiler produces code for a PowerPC Macintosh, but the compiler itself runs on a 680X0 Macintosh. A native compiler executes on and generates code for the same platform. A cross compiler can be very useful to an application developer who does not yet have a target platform. This allows applications to be ported to a new platform before the new platform is generally available.

Compilers are often bundled along with tools including assemblers, debuggers and linkers in a framework with an editor and GUI. This is referred to as either an *integrated development environment* (IDE) or a *software development kit* (SDK).

Object code is produced in different formats, depending upon the platform. Some terms you may see include XCOFF(AIX/UNIX), PEF(APPLE), ELF, extended ELF and DWARF.

Following is a list of available and soon-to-be-announced compilers:

- C/C++
    - IBM: C Set ++
    - Motorola: Optimizing C Compiler for the PowerPC 6XX Microprocessor
    - Absoft: C/C++ Compiler
    - Apple: C/C++ Compiler
    - Metrowerks: C/C++ Compiler
    - Symantec: C++ 7.0 Compiler
    - DiabData: C/C++ Compiler
    - Metaware: C/C++ Cross Compiler
    - Watcom: C/C++ 10.0
- Fortran
    - IBM: XL Fortran Compiler
    - Motorola: Optimizing Fortran Compiler for the PowerPC 6XX Microprocessor
    - Absoft: Fortran 77 Compiler
    - LS: Fortran
    - DiabData: Fortran Compiler
- Pascal
    - IBM: XL Pascal Compiler
    - Metrowerks: Pascal
    - LS: Pascal

Debugger: Debuggers can generally be classified according to the type of source code they inspect and by the framework they use to interact with the target debugger.

- By Source Code Inspection
    - Source-Level Debugger

The symbolic debugger allows a software developer to set breakpoints, step execution, examine and alter data according to type, and trace control flow for source code written in a high-level language such as C and C++. It provides an effective way for isolating errors in C/C++ coded portions of the operating system, translators, and applications.

  – Register-Level Debugger

    The register-level debugger is the assembly equivalent of symbolic debugging for C/C++ sources. All programmer-visible resources, such as all registers and memory, are accessible using this debugger. As in the symbolic debugger, breakpoints, execution single step, control trace and formatted data are provided. Here, however, instructions are disassembled to a mnemonic representation rather than mapped back to corresponding source code lines.

• By Debugger Interaction Framework

  – Native Debugger

    A native debugger itself executes on the same platform as that of its target debugger.

  – Remote Target Debugger

    A symbolic or register-level debugger which resides on a stable host system and controls code through a software monitor executing on a remote victim system is considered a remote target debugger. Typically, these debuggers assume communications services are present and stable on both systems such as a serial link or network protocol. They are thus distinguished from umbilical debuggers, which do not require the victim to provide communications services or sufficient stability to run monitor.

Following is a list of debuggers available in the market or planned for release:

• IBM: RiscWatch Debugger

• Absoft: FX Multi-Language Debugger

Debuggers are usually included in compilers or SDKs.

PowerPC Software Development Kits: Software development kits are most often used by application developers in order to either port code or develop new code to run on PowerPC systems. These developers typically write code in a high-level language, although portions may be rewritten in assembly language for maximum performance. The developer then uses a compiler, assembler, and linker to produce modules which are loaded by the operating system and executed on the system. The debugger aids in isolating errors in the code, and the code profiler can be used to study the performance of the applications.

An SDK is a framework in which individual software development tools are often bundled. Typical components of an SDK include one or more compilers, an assembler, linker, debugger, code profiler, browser, and a text editor. SDKs customarily provide a uniform interface to access all components, and may add inter-tool communication so that, for example, a compiler syntax error would be reflected by placing the text editor at the source code line of the offending statement.

A compiler is used to translate high-level language source code to object code.

An assembler translates machine instructions represented by mnemonics (assembly language) to object code. It facilitates access to the full processor instruction set. It is frequently used to code routines which access architectural features which are not visible from a high-level language, and to manage performance-critical routines. Both assemblers and compilers can exist in native or cross form. A cross assembler differs from native assembler in that the assembler itself runs on a platform which is different from the platform of its target object. A native assembler or compiler generates code for the same platform that it runs on.

A linker supports the assembler and compiler by resolving symbols external to the object modules generated. This allows programs to utilize libraries and make calls to external routines.

A debugger allows a software developer to set breakpoints, step execution, examine and alter data, and trace control flow through a program. This can be done at the source code level with a symbolic debugger, or at the assembly level using a register-level debugger.

A code profiler provides statistical analysis of program execution. Typical measurements that are provided for each subroutine invoked include the number of calls made, percentage of total program execution time spent in the function body, and an estimate of average time spent for each call.

A browser is a post-compilation static analysis tool that a developer can use to view the relationship between source code entities such as classes, functions, and files.

Following is a list of available or soon-to-be-announced software development kits:
- IBM: POWERbench
- IBM: C Set ++
- Apple: SDK on RISC
- Metrowerks: Codewarrior
- Symantec: C++ Cross Development Toolkit
- DiabData: C/C++ Compiler

- Cardence: System Workbench

5.2.3 Development Support

5.2.3.1 IBM Power Series Developer's ToolBox Program
This program is designed for qualified U.S. commercial developers who plan to port products to or develop and market products for IBM Power Series and operating systems. This program is also intended for internal developers who plan to port internally used software or hardware to or develop internally used software or hardware for IBM Power Series and operating systems. Those operating systems include IBM OS/2 Warp Connect (PowerPC Edition), AIX Version 4 for clients, Solaris, and Windows NT Workstation operating system.

Contact point

IBM Corporation
IBM Developer's ToolBox Program, 3200 Windy Hill Road - WG14C, Atlanta, GA 30339
- 1-800-627-8363, Fax : (404)835-9444

5.2.3.2 Porting Center
A Windows NT porting center is available to help developers who are interested in porting their products to this platform. The center provides:

- Technical support to OEMs, IHVs, and ISVs who are producing systems and products for the Windows NT on the PowerPC Reference Platform specification environment

- Assistance in evaluating and correcting performance issues

- Monitors performance of Windows NT on the PowerPC vs. other platforms

---
Contact point

- 1-800-803-0110 or 1-206-889-9011
Internet : winntppc@vnet.ibm.com.

5.2.3.3 The POWER Team
The POWER Team is a program developed for POWER and PowerPC system hardware and software developers to help them build and grow their product in the AIX marketplace.

POWER Team members will receive technical, business and marketing information on a regular basis. The following support is given to participants:

- Porting assistance

- Consulting for design reviews, performance tuning

- Online information: Electronic bulletin board, Q & A database, field television network educational broadcasts

- POWER and PowerPC conferences

Contact point

IBM Corporation
Software Vendor Operations, 472 Wheelers Farms Road, Milford, CT 06460
- (800)627-8363, Fax : (203)783-7669
Internet : AIXPROGS@RHQVM21.VNET.IBM.COM

Chapter 6. PowerPC - Hardware and Product Overview

This chapter concentrates on the IBM Power Series. We cover hardware architectures and design and then have a look at the systems.

6.1 IBM Power Series Hardware Architecture

The IBM Power Series systems offer the next generation of performance for demanding client/server environments in large and medium businesses, as well as in government and higher education. These systems offer you the open-ended performance of PowerPC technology that protects your investment today as well as tomorrow. You will be able to choose among the leading, stable, robust, advanced 32-bit operating systems such as AIX, OS/2, Windows NT, and Solaris.

PowerPC promises new technologies that are both practical and pervasive. These technologies include subsystems such as graphics, multimedia, speech recognition, pen and collaborative computing. PowerPC will also provide the user with exciting new user interfaces.

In order to understand the IBM Power Series, it is necessary to first have a look at the typical hardware design. This design is shown in Figure 6-1 on page 6-2.

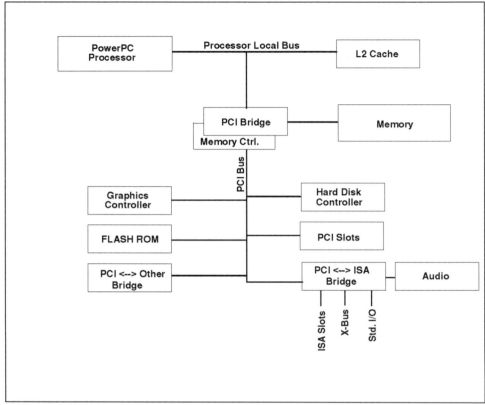

Figure 6-1. *Typical IBM Power Series Design*

The general hardware design is also explained in 4.1, "PowerPC Reference Platform Specification" on page 4-1 and 4.3, "The New PowerPC Microprocessor Hardware Reference Platform" on page 4-9.

We will briefly look at the main subsystems that contribute to a PowerPC Personal System before moving on to the new products as systems in their own right.

6.1.1 Processor Subsystem

As could be inferred from the name, this subsystem contains the processor(s). The processor operates on the instructions and data fed to it by the applications and operating system. In order for this subsystem to comply with the PowerPC Reference Platform specification, it has to meet the requirements described in this specification.

6.1.2 Memory Subsystem

The memory subsystem can be subdivided into six systems. These systems are:

1. System Memory

   The portion of memory where executable instructions reside is referred to as the system memory. Systems must have at least 8MB of system memory that must be expandable to a minimum of 16MB. It is strongly recommended that this memory will be either parity checking, or Error Checking and Correcting (ECC).

2. System ROM

   Power-on firmware, boot firmware, as well as additional data needed by the system is stored in the System ROM. System ROM will typically be implemented by the use of ROM, EPROM or FLASH ROM. All systems must include a System ROM.

3. Non-Volatile Memory

   Non-Volatile memory (NVRAM) is used to store system configuration. It is also used as an error indicator across system boots. A typical system contains 4KB of NVRAM that must maintain its state in the absence of system power.

4. I/O Memory

   This is the area in the memory map that refers to the addresses where I/O devices reside. Some examples of memory I/O devices are graphics and communication peripherals. I/O memory can exist on the system expansion bus, but remains part of the I/O bus and is typically not cached. Although I/O memory can be located on the primary processor bus, it will only participate in the hardware-managed coherency protocol if other ports do not interfere in the same area.

5. System I/O

   The system I/O is the area in the memory map that handles the addressing and communications for I/O devices.

6. External Cache

   This is the cache that resides between any on-chip processor caches or Level 1 (L1) and system memory. External cache is typically referred to as level 2 (L2), and enhances system performance further.

   New processors like the PowerPC 601 can execute up to five operations every 15 nanoseconds. The challenge is therefore to keep the processor filled with enough instructions so that it may operate at maximum capacity. This is achieved by using external cache.

   Cache is a small amount of very fast memory that holds the next few thousand instructions and data for the processor. Due to the sequential nature of the instruction stream of most programs, it is very likely that the next instruction and data to be processed will be found in the cache. It can thus be executed quickly without requiring access to the slower main memory.

6.1.3 Storage Subsystems

According to the PowerPC Reference Platform specification, the following subsystems and interfaces will be used:

- Hard file

  Every system must either have a hard file or have the capability to access a hard file. The minimum size for an internal hard file is 120MB, but 200MB is strongly recommended as the minimum capacity. Hard files can be attached through a direct connection using SCSI or IDE, or through networking and expansion adapters.

- Diskette

  Diskette drives must support the 3.5-inch, 1.44MB modified frequency modulation (MFM) format. Optional features, such as electronic eject through software control, can be added.

- CD-ROM

  CD-ROM drives included in these systems must at least conform to the ISO 9660 standard. Drives should also be of the double-speed variety, capable of transferring at least 300KB per second. CD-ROM connection may be achieved through either IDE or SCSI.

- SCSI

  The small computer system interface (SCSI) is an ANSI standard specification that is widely used as a peripheral bus. Systems that implement SCSI must comply to the ANSI Standard X3.131-1990 for SCSI-2. The interface will mainly be used to support hard files and CD-ROMs, but could also be used to support scanners, tapes and optical drives. Additionally it could be used to attach RAID-based storage systems.

- IDE

  Integrated device electronics (IDE) is an optional interface for hard files. Systems implementing IDE should comply with the X3.221 ANSI Standard. As enhanced IDE becomes a standard, it is recommended that systems use it as the standard interface, hence allowing for support of devices with capacity above 520MB.

6.1.4 Human Interface Subsystem

The human interface subsystem includes the following devices:

- Alphanumeric Input Device

Every system must include an alphanumeric input device. The most common realization of this is the directly attached keyboard. Examples are the 101/102-key keyboard.

- Pointing Device

When a system has a directly attached or built-in keyboard, it must also have a directly attached or built-in pointing device. Examples of pointing devices include a mouse, Track Point II, digitizer tablet and touch screen.

- Audio

In order to conform to the PowerPC Personal System minimum design requirement, a system must include audio capability. The audio subsystem must consist of at least two analog-to-digital input channels and at least two digital-to-analog output channels. These channels must support sample widths of at least 16 bits. Sampling rates of 22.05 and 44.1KHz must be supported.

The audio subsystems include a soft digital signal processor (DSP) implementation. Traditional audio adapters use a hardware chip to handle DSP. Soft DSP is obtained by the intensive floating point and vector arithmetic capabilities of the PowerPC processor. Additional high interrupt rates coupled with low interrupt latency and a seamless interface to the data I/O stream assist in this implementation.

The PowerPC systems are therefore very well equipped for voice annotation, text-to-audio conversion as well as compression and expansion of digital data streams.

- Graphics

Built-in graphics subsystems should support a resolution of 640x480 and 256 colors as an absolute minimum. It is however recommendable to support higher resolutions of at least 1024x768, and color depth of 8, 16 and 24 bits. In 1995, systems will support Bi-Endian graphics operation and system software must therefore be able to access the graphics buffer in either Endian format.

6.1.5 Real-Time Clock Subsystem

A system must include a real-time clock (RTC). The RTC must be able to operate in the absence of system power. It must provide the necessary information to determine the year, month, day, hour, minute and second.

6.1.6 Connectivity Subsystems

In this section we will focus our attention on the major connectivity devices of the PowerPC Personal System. These devices are:

- Serial

Every system should include at least one serial port. This port must be implemented using EIA/TIA-232-E signal compatibility. A nine-pin D-shell male connector will be used. The port must support asynchronous protocol with baud rates up to at least 19.2Kbps.

- Parallel

  Although not essential, it is highly recommended to include one parallel port. If the port is included then it must be compliant with the IEEE P1284 standard specification. The port should also support the extended capabilities port (ECP) compatibility mode. Although the Centronics interface is used by most "IBM-compatible" personal computers, the interface has never been formalized.

- Network

  For low-end network communications use LocalTalk (the standard Macintosh serial port), conforming to EIA-422-A. LocalTalk is compatible with the SCC 8530 controller and is defined by industry standards and protocols. Use Ethernet or token-ring where higher performance is required. When using Ethernet, conform to the IEEE 802.3 standard. Token-ring implementation adheres to the IEEE 802.5 standard.

6.1.7 Bus Types

The PowerPC Personal System supports a large variety of bus types. In theory all the popular bus architectures (that is, ISA, EISA, Micro Channel, PCI, VESA and PCMCIA) can be supported. The current PowerPC Personal System implements:

- ISA
- PCMCIA
- PCI

ISA bus systems must comply with the IEEE definition of ISA. Systems that are plug-and-play enabled must conform to plug-and-play specifications. All plug-and-play devices must be uniquely identifiable, state the services they provide and the resources they require. It must also identify the driver that supports it and be software configurable.

PCMCIA implementation is the 68-pin card and socket version, compatible with Release 2.x. The PCMCIA software architecture has two key elements, namely socket services and card services. Socket services is a hardware-dependent interface and is therefore supplied by the system vendor. The purpose of socket services is to mask the socket's actual hardware implementation from higher-level software components that utilize it. Card services is a software layer that sits above socket services, coordinating access among the cards, the sockets and system resources such as interrupts and the memory map. It is the responsibility of the operating system vendor to supply the card services extensions. Card services accesses cards via socket services. The card drivers (enablers) interact with the card via card services. It is the responsibility of the PC card vendor to provide card enablers (drivers). In general, card services is operating system-dependent.

The *PCI* bus was originally designed to provide the Pentium processor with all the bandwidth it needed. Because it was not tied to the Intel family it is very suitable for attachment to the PowerPC platform. PCI is a full 64-bit processor independent bus. This is achieved through the design concept that isolates the PCI bus completely from the processor and memory bus. Major advantages of the PCI bus are its ability to provide automatic configuration and the resolution of hardware conflicts. Refer to the PCI technical specification for more information about the PCI implementation.

6.1.8 Controllers

- Universal Micro Control Unit (UMCU)

  The UMCU is the very basic function center of the system. It is the only logical hardware that is alive even when the power is switched off but still connected to the external source. The UMCU manages basic power functions. It provides functions in keyboard control, system power control, power management event control and other peripheral device control.

  The UMCU communicates with the system microprocessor by message passing and event notification through a message block. This block is made up of registers implemented in the extended I/O controller.

- Native I/O controller

  A National Semiconducter SuperI/O (PC87322) is used and contains the following function blocks.

  - Diskette drive controller
  - Serial port controller
  - Parallel port controller
  - IDE interface

- Extended I/O controller

  The Extended I/O controller is a sweep of several different devices. Some of these device are used in all the products while other are customized to a specific system for specific functions. The following functions are provided:

  - Keyboard/mouse interface controller
  - C2 EEPROM interface controller
  - UMCU controller support
  - NVRAM interface control
  - RTC/CMOS interface control
  - IC DRAM card presence detect

- Audio CODEC interface control
- FDD support
- SCSI support
- LED indicators
- System X-data bus buffer control
- System address 8XX register interface

- PCI Bridge and Memory Controller

  This controller consists of two modules that act together to make the connection between the processor, memory and PCI buses. The functions of the PCI Bridge and memory Controller are as follows:

  - SIMM memory controller
  - Bridge from PowerPC processor to PCI bus
  - Burst or single beat access from CPU
  - Burst or single beat access from PCI
  - PCI and PowerPC processor bus arbitration
  - Error reporting to the PowerPC processor
  - Endian mode switching

- PCI-ISA Bridge Controller (Intel 82378ZB System I/O)

  This controller provides the ISA bus bridge as well as a host of other features. These features are:

  - 20MHz PCI bus operation
  - PCI bus interface
  - PCI bus arbitration
  - PCI configurations registers
  - ISA bus interface
  - High performance PCI attached IDE interface
  - X-Data bus support
  - 82C54 programmable interval timer
  - 82C59 programmable interrupt controller
  - 16-bit BIOS timer
  - Test support logic

  The PCI-ISA bridge decodes PCI cycles for selected addresses and unclaimed PCI cycles for the ISA bus.

- Power Management Controller

  The power management controller is derived from the IBM ThinkPad product line. In addition to power management, the controller also handles other planar logic, that results in cost savings. The following functions are provided by the Power Management controller:

  - Power management support

- PCI FLASH ROM interface
- PCI arbitration
- PCI bus operation up to 33MHz

6.2 The IBM Power Series Product Line

The invention of the PowerPC processors has opened the door for IBM to design an exciting new range of Personal Computers. These systems will be known as the IBM Power Series. The family consists of both desktop and mobile systems.

The new IBM Power Series family of products represent the evolution of the personal computer into the professional workstation, utilizing the best from both worlds. Powerful, flexible and competitively priced, the Power Personal System family is designed to address user's most demanding computing requirements. With the performance provided, the systems can effectively run both 16-bit and 32-bit operating systems and applications. With true multitasking, the IBM Power Series concurrently run multiple programs, including such processor-intensive applications as desktop publishing, spreadsheets, database applications, presentation graphics and multimedia.

We will now move on to a short description of the current models.

6.2.1 IBM Personal Computer Power Series 830 and 850

The IBM Personal Computer Power Series 830 and 850 systems redefine desktop computing to new levels of system price/performance. These desktop performers combine the performance characteristics of RISC technology (Reduced Instruction Set Computers) with the price characteristics of state-of-the-art Personal Computer technology. They provide leadership technology, advanced industrial design, and IBM quality, service and support.

Figure   6-2. *IBM Personal Computer Power Series 830 and 850*

In addition, the IBM Personal Computer Power Series 830 and 850 systems include a rich, visually stunning "out-of-box" software. This provides an introduction to the system, its capabilites and strengths, which should help familiarize users with the system and increase productivity.

The IBM Personal Computer Power Series 830 and 850 system technology encompasses:

- PowerPC 604 microprocessors
- PCI/ISA bus architectures
- Processor upgrades to provide growth and help to protect investment
- Enhanced PCI local bus IDE controller
- The ability to expand memory from 16MB to 192MB and internal hard disk storage from 540MB to 3GB
- Standard business audio sound system that enables stereo in/out stereo headphone, and microphone

The Personal Computer Power Series includes two specific products:

- The Personal Computer Power Series 830 is a 3-slot/3-bay space saver design.
- The Personal Computer Power Series 850 is a 5-slot/5-bay desktop design.

All the IBM Personal Computer Power Series 830 and 850 systems come with a three-year warranty.

Whether you are selecting these new systems to run the existing personal productivity applications or to develop new line-of-business applications, your requirements are varied. The IBM Personal Computer Power Series 830 and 850 systems make getting the right system for your unique requirements easy, by offering the customer a build-to-order system. This building block approach allows customers to configure the system to meet their specific needs.

The IBM Personal Computer Power Series 830 and 850 systems include an operating system of choice. When possible, the operating system will be installed on the hard disk. The operating systems that will be supported by the IBM Personal Computer Power Series 830 and 850 include:

- OS/2 Warp Connect (PowerPC Edition)
- Windows NT Workstation 3.51 (PowerPC Edition)
- AIX Version 4 for Clients
- Solaris (PowerPC Edition)

Systems are also available with no operating system installed

6.2.1.1 System Characteristics

Following is a short description of the IBM Personal Computer Power Series 830 and 850 technical specifications:

Microprocessor

- Power Series 830: PowerPC 604 100MHz
- Power Series 850: PowerPC 604 100MHz, 120MHz or 133MHz

L2 cache

- 100MHz and 120MHz: 256KB standard, 512KB optional
- 133MHz: 512KB standard

Bus architecture

- PCI local bus
- Enhanced IDE controller

Memory

- Parity memory for data integrity
- 16MB memory minimum
- 192 maximum (installed in matching pairs of 70ns SIMMs)

Communications

- Standard PCI local-bus-attached 10BaseT Ethernet on the system board

Integrated audio

- Full 16-bit stereo business audio

- FM synthesis for music and sound effects

- Built-in speaker

- IBM Personal Microphone (for speech recognition and other voice applications)

Video graphics support

- Standard: PCI SVGA local-bus graphics with 2MB DRAM

- Three optional high-performance adapter cards:

    - IBM S15 Graphics Adapter, a 2MB VRAM-based 24-bit graphics adapter with integrated video coprocessor (motion video acceleration)

    - IBM H10 Graphics Adapter, a 4MB VRAM-based 24-bit PCI graphics adapter with integrated video coprocessor (motion video acceleration)

    - IBM POWER GXT150P Graphics Adapter, a 8-bit, 3MB advanced PCI graphics adapter (3-D capable)

- Optional IBM Video Capture Enhancement adapter for use with S15 or H10 only

CD-ROM drive

- Built-in 680MB quad-speed drive, Kodak Photo-CD, multisession-capable

IDE hard drives supported

- IDE 540MB, 728MB or 1GB

- Power Series 850: Up to three internal drives supported for up to 3GB storage

Optional SCSI-2 subsystems supported (Power Series 850 only)

- 540MB, 1GB and 2GB hard drives

- Quad-speed SCSI-2 CD-ROM drive

- 4/10GB 4mm SCSI-2 tape drive

- Support for up to 5GB internally

- Requires IBM SCSI-2 Fast/Wide PCI adapter card and cable

Diskette drives

- Standard: 1.44MB 3.5-inch diskette drive

- Optional: 1.2MB 5.25-inch diskette drive

Monitors supported

- IBM P50 - 13.6-inch diagonal viewable screen size

- IBM P70 - 15.9-inch diagonal viewable screen size

- IBM P200 - 19.1-inch diagonal viewable screen size

- IBM P201 - 19.1-inch diagonal viewable screen size

- IBM 17S/S Sight and Sound monitor - 16.0-inch diagonal viewable screen size

- IBM 952X family of monitors

Standard I/O ports

- SVGA monitor port

- 2 serial ports

- 1 enhanced parallel port

- Microphone and speaker jacks

- Audio line in/line out

- MIDI/joystick port

- Ethernet 10BaseT

Let us now have a look at the different models of the Personal Computer Power Series.

6.2.1.2 Personal Computer Power Series 830

Figure 6-3 on page 6-14 shows the design diagram of the Personal Computer Power Series 830.

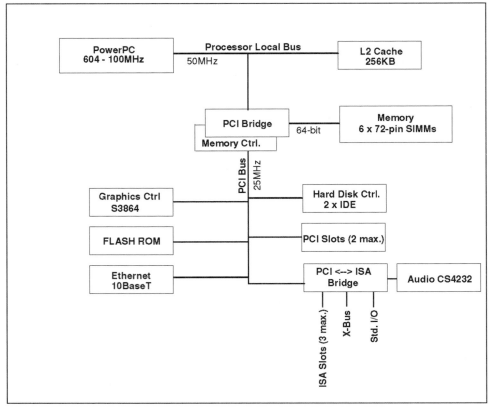

Figure   6-3. *Personal Computer Power Series 830 Design Diagram*

The following table provides an overview of the main characteristics of the Personal Computer Power Series 830:

Table   6-1 (Page 1 of 2). *Personal Computer Power Series 830 Characteristics*

System		Personal Computer Power Series 830
Processor	standard	604 - 100MHz, 256KB L2 cache
	upgrade	processor socket
Memory	std. / max.	16MB / 192MB
	sockets	6 x 72-pin, 4 free (install SIMMs in pairs!)
	expansion	4, 8, 16, 32MB parity SIMMs, 70ns

System		Personal Computer Power Series 830
Storage	bays	3 (0 free)
	controller	1 x Enhanced IDE (2 drives max.)
	diskette	3.5-inch 1.44MB, media sense
	std. disk	540MB min. (IDE)
	std. CD-ROM	Quad-speed (IDE)
Human Interface	keyboard/mouse	yes / yes
	audio	Crystal Semiconductor CS4232
	graphics	S3 864 DSP, 2MB DRAM
Connectivity	serial / parallel	2 x 9-pin / 1 x enhanced parallel
	network	10BaseT Ethernet (RJ45 twisted pair)
Expansion buses		1 x dedicated ISA 1/2 size
		2 x shared ISA / PCI

6.2.1.3 Personal Computer Power Series 850

Figure 6-4 on page 6-16 shows the design diagram of the Personal Computer Power Series 850 100MHz.

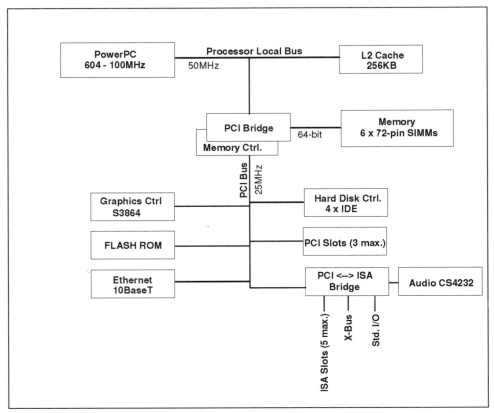

Figure *6-4. Personal Computer Power Series 850 100MHz Design Diagram*

The design diagram of the Personal Computer Power Series 850 120MHz is depicted in Figure 6-5 on page 6-17, and for the Personal Computer Power Series 850 133MHz in Figure 6-6 on page 6-18. Note that the design for the three different models differs only in the speed of the processor, the processor local bus, and the PCI bus, and in the fact that the 133MHz version has 512KB level2 cache standard.

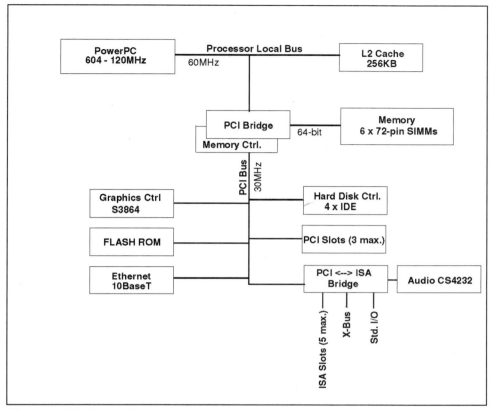

Figure 6-5. *Personal Computer Power Series 850 120MHz Design Diagram*

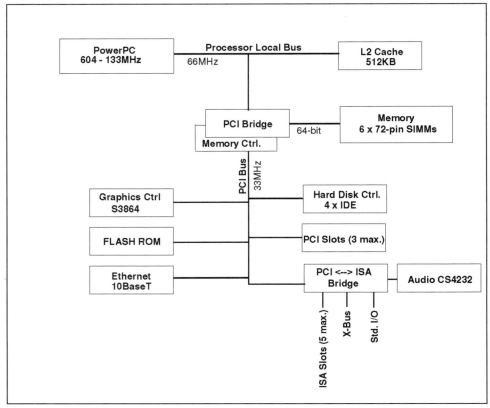

Figure   6-6. Personal Computer Power Series 850 133MHz Design Diagram

The following table provides an overview of the main characteristics of the Personal
Computer Power Series 850:

Table 6-2 (Page 1 of 2). *Personal Computer Power Series 850 Characteristics*		
System		**Personal Computer Power Series 850**
Processor	standard	604 - 100MHz, 256KB L2 cache
		604 - 120MHz, 256KB L2 cache
		604 - 133MHz, 512KB L2 cache
	upgrade	processor socket
Memory	std. / max.	16MB / 192MB
	sockets	6 x 72-pin, 4 free (install SIMMs in pairs!)
	expansion	4, 8, 16, 32MB parity SIMMs, 70ns

System		Personal Computer Power Series 850
Storage	bays	5 (2 free)
	controller	2 x Enhanced IDE (4 drives max.)
	diskette	3.5-inch 1.44MB, media sense
	std. disk	540MB min. (IDE)
	std. CD-ROM	Quad-speed (IDE)
Human Interface	keyboard/mouse	yes / yes
	audio	Crystal Semiconductor CS4232
	graphics	S3 864 DSP, 2MB DRAM
Connectivity	serial / parallel	2 x 9-pin / 1 x enhanced parallel
	network	10BaseT Ethernet (RJ45 twisted pair)
Expansion buses		2 x dedicated ISA full, 1 x dedicated ISA 1/2 size
		2 x shared ISA / PCI

6.2.1.4 Riser Cards

The following two figures show the riser cards used in the IBM Personal Computer Power Series 830 and 850 systems. The 3-slot riser card is used in the Personal Computer Power Series 830, the 5-slot riser card in the Personal Computer Power Series 850.

Riser cards are plugged into the system board vertically and provide a number of expansion slots for both PCI and ISA bus. The 3-slot riser card shown in Figure 6-7 on page 6-20 provides one dedicated ISA card slot and two shared PCI/ISA card slots. You can use a maximum of 3 slots at a time. Each of the shared card slots can accommodate one ISA card or one PCI card at a time, but not both at the same time. So, the first *or* the second slot from the bottom can be used, and the third *or* the fourth slot from the bottom. You cannot use the first *and* second or the third *and* fourth slot from the bottom.

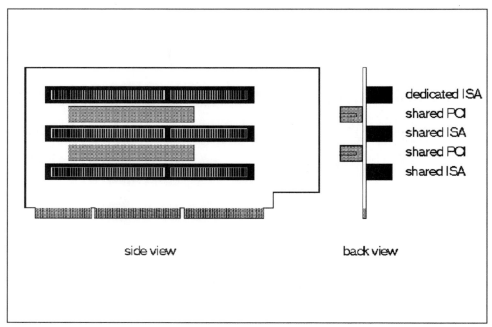

dedicated ISA
shared PCI
shared ISA
shared PCI
shared ISA

side view   back view

Figure   6-7. 3-Slot Riser Card

Figure 6-8 on page 6-21 shows the 5-slot riser card used in the Personal Computer
Power Series 850. This card provides three dedicated ISA card slots and, as in the 3-slot
riser card, two shared PIC/ISA card slots. You can use a maximum of 5 slots at a time.
The same restrictions apply for the shared slots as on the 3-slot riser card.

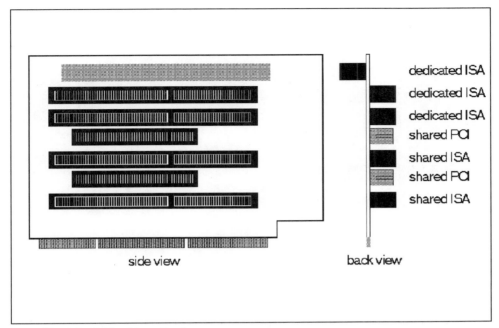

side view   back view

dedicated ISA
dedicated ISA
dedicated ISA
shared PCI
shared ISA
shared PCI
shared ISA

Figure 6-8. 5-Slot Riser Card

6.2.2 IBM ThinkPad Power Series 820 and 850

With the IBM ThinkPad Power Series 820 and 850, you can put the power of
RISC-based computing on the job anywhere. The PowerPC 603e microprocessor
provides a leap in industry-leadership application performance through its 100MHz
speed, 32KB Level 1 cache and 256KB Level 2 cache support.

Figure *6-9.* *IBM ThinkPad Power Series 820 and 850*

At the same time, you get the innovative features you've come to expect with an IBM ThinkPad: large, state-of-the-art TFT displays with glare-reducing Black Matrix technology and IBM's industry-leading integrated TrackPoint III pointing device. The operating systems that will be supported by the IBM ThinkPad Power Series 820 and 850 include:

- OS/2 Warp Connect (PowerPC Edition)
- Windows NT Workstation 3.51 (PowerPC Edition)
- AIX Version 4 for Clients
- Solaris (PowerPC Edition)

Systems are also available with no operating system installed

The IBM ThinkPad Power Series 820 and 850 both come with integrated 16-bit stereo business audio, internal stereo speakers, a built-in microphone and an internal dual-speed CD-ROM drive.

6.2.2.1 System Characteristics

Following is a short description of the IBM ThinkPad Power Series 820 and 850 technical specifications:

Processor

- PowerPC 603e 100MHz with 32KB L1 internal cache

- 256KB L2 cache

Bus architecture

- Power Series 820: 32-bit memory
- Power Series 850: 64-bit memory

Memory

- Parity memory for data integrity
- Power Series 820:
    - 16MB or 32MB base memory
    - 48MB maximum via sockets for 8MB or 16MB Memory Modules
- Power Series 850:
    - 16MB or 32MB base memory
    - 80MB or 96MB maximum via two sockets for 4MB, 8MB, 16MB or 32MB IC DRAM cards (installed in matching pairs)

Display

- SVGA
    - 10.4-inch (measured diagonally) active matrix TFT color LCD
    - sidelit
    - 65,536 colors at 800x600 resolution
    - 110:1 contrast ratio
- VGA
    - 10.4-inch (measured diagonally) active matrix TFT color LCD
    - sidelit
    - 65,536 colors at 640x480 resolution
    - 100:1 contrast ratio
- Black matrix technology for superior viewability in bright light

Video graphics

- PCI local bus
- IBM ThinkPad Power Series G10 Graphics
- Motion video, NTSC in/out and PAL in (optional on Power Series 820)
- Power Series 850: Snap-in video camera (optional)

- Simultaneous display of LCD and external SVGA monitor

Audio

- Integrated 16-bit business audio
- Built-in microphone and stereo speakers
- IBM Personal Microphone (for speech recognition and other voice applications)

Storage

- Removable 540MB, 810MB, or 1.2GB SCSI-2 hard drives
- Internal SCSI-2 double-speed removable CD-ROM drive
- Internal/external 3.5-inch 1.44MB diskette drive
- Support for optional 1GB or 2GB external hard drives

Expandability

- PCMCIA slots for two Type I/II cards or one Type III card
- 120-pin ISA bus connector
- External SCSI-2 port

Standard I/O Interfaces

- SVGA external display port (supports monitors up to 1024x768 resolution)
- Enhanced parallel port
- Serial port
- External keyboard/mouse/numeric keypad port
- External diskette drive port
- SCSI-2 port
- Audio line in/out (Power Series 850 only)
- Headphone and microphone jacks
- Motion video in (NTSC and PAL) and out (NTSC) jacks (optional on Power Series 820)

Keyboard

- Integrated TrackPoint III pointing device with QuickStop response and drag lock buttons
- 85 full-size keys
- Full key travel

Power supply

- Rechargeable NiMH Battery Pack

- Battery life can range from 2.0 to 5.0 hours

- 1.5-hour internal quick charge in power-off or suspend mode, 2.0-hour during operation

- 50W external worldwide AC adapter

- Optional Travel Quick Charger (Power Series 820)

- Optional Quick Charger (Power Series 850)

6.2.2.2 ThinkPad Power Series 820

The ThinkPad Power Series 820 provides world-class performance with a PowerPC 603e 100MHz microprocessor in a small, lightweight system that can be battery or AC powered.

Multitasking capability and the choice of high-performance, 32-bit operating systems make the ThinkPad Power Series 820 an ideal general business solution for mobile, field and office professionals. The system is well-suited for extremely demanding computer uses. Its innovative design offers palm-rest space, built-in stereo speakers and integrated CD-ROM.

Models of the ThinkPad Power Series 820 with the optional G10 Graphics with Motion Video Adapter can send and receive composite video. Motion video can be input from a NTSC or PAL camcorder, displayed on an NTSC television monitor, or recorded on an NTSC VCR.

In addition to motion video I/O capabilities, the ThinkPad Power Series 820 has full multimedia support with built-in audio and integrated CD-ROM capability. All this capability comes in a sleek seven-pound system that meets the requirements for U.S. Energy Star compliance.

With its new supporting options, the ThinkPad Power Series 820 delivers a feature-packed, powerful, flexible, expandable mobile computer that is designed to address the most demanding computing requirements.

Figure 6-10 on page 6-26 shows the ThinkPad Power Series 820 design diagram.

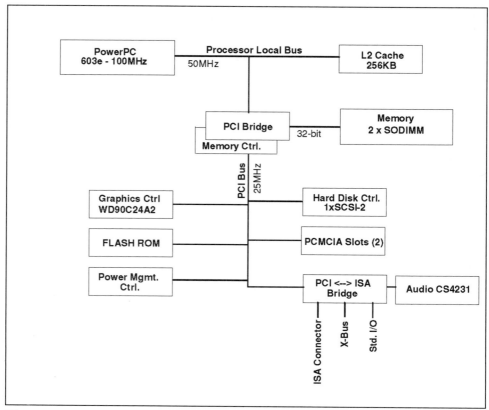

Figure 6-10. *ThinkPad Power Series 820 Design Diagram*

A summary of the characteristics of ThinkPad Power Series 820 is given in Table 6-3.

Table 6-3 (Page 1 of 2). *ThinkPad Power Series 820 Characteristics*

System		ThinkPad Power Series 820
Processor	standard	603e - 100MHz, 256KB L2 cache
	upgrade	CPU card
Memory	std. / max.	16MB / 48MB
	sockets	3 x 72-pin SODIMM
	expansion	8, 16MB SODIMM

Table 6-3 (Page 2 of 2). *ThinkPad Power Series 820 Characteristics*

System		ThinkPad Power Series 820
Storage	bays	1 x disk drive, 1 x CD-ROM or diskette
	controller	1 x SCSI-2 fast
	diskette	3.5-inch 1.44MB, media sense, external
	std. disk	540MB / 810MB / 1.2GB removable (SCSI)
	std. CD-ROM	Double speed (SCSI)
Human Interface	keyboard/mouse	yes / TrackPoint III
	audio	Crystal Semiconductor CS4231
	graphics	Western Digital WD90C24A2, 1MB DRAM
	display	10.4-inch TFT color LCD, 640x480
		10.4-inch TFT color LCD, 800x600
Connectivity	serial / parallel	1 x 9-pin / 1 x enhanced parallel
	network	none
Expansion buses		PCMCIA: 2 x Type I or II, or 1 x Type III
Physical	dimensions	297 x 210 x 56 mm - 11.7 x 8.3 x 2.2 inches
	weight	2.8 kg (6.16 lbs) with battery
		3.0 kg (6.64 lbs) with battery and FDD
		3.4 kg (7.53 lbs) with battery and CD-ROM

6.2.2.3 ThinkPad Power Series 850

With the body of a ThinkPad and the soul of a PowerPC, the ThinkPad Power Series 850 allows you to carry collaborative and conversational computing wherever you go. This premium-function mobile product extends IBM's ThinkPad family, with advanced features and blazing performance provided by its PowerPC 603e 100MHz processor.

All models of ThinkPad Power Series 850 take mobile productivity one step further by offering a standard G10 Graphics with Motion Video Adapter for video I/O, a snap-in video camera option, and voice-over-data capability using standard modems, plus the floating point unit of the PowerPC 603e.

These features, plus such additional built-in functions as a multisession CD-ROM and audio I/O with microphone and stereo speakers, provide a system that is ideal for advanced collaboration and multimedia applications. Combine these features with those that have made the ThinkPad world-class - brilliant active matrix 800x600 Black Matrix displays, the TrackPoint III pointing device, PCMCIA expandability, and user-removable 1.2GB hard disk drives, and you have a product that is ready for your applications today and in the future. All this capability is wrapped in an award-winning, sleek, eight-pound system that meets the requirements for U.S. Energy Star compliance.

The design diagram of the ThinkPad Power Series 850 is shown in Figure 6-11.

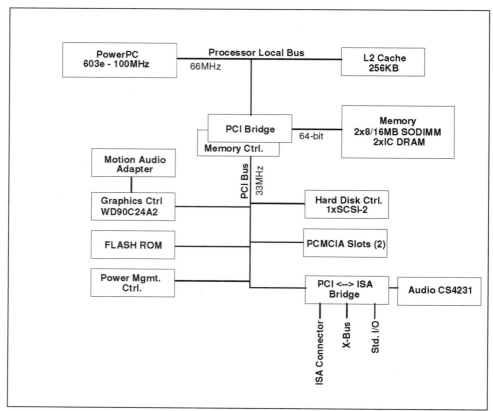

Figure **6-11.** *ThinkPad Power Series 850 Design Diagram*

Table 6-4 gives an overview of the ThinkPad Power Series 850 main characteristics.

Table **6-4** *(Page 1 of 2).* *ThinkPad Power Series 850 Characteristics*		
System		**ThinkPad Power Series 850**
Processor	standard	603e - 100MHz, 256KB L2 cache
	upgrade	CPU card

Table 6-4 (Page 2 of 2). ThinkPad Power Series 850 Characteristics

System		ThinkPad Power Series 850
Memory	std. / max.	16MB / 80MB or 32MB / 96MB
	sockets	2 x 88-pin IC DRAM (install pair!)
	expansion	4, 8, 16, 32MB IC DRAM, 70ns, parity
Storage	bays	1 x disk drive, 1 x CD-ROM or diskette
	controller	1 x SCSI-2 fast
	diskette	3.5-inch 1.44MB, media sense, external
	std. disk	540MB / 810MB / 1.2GB removable (SCSI)
	std. CD-ROM	Double speed (SCSI)
Human Interface	keyboard/mouse	yes / TrackPoint III
	audio	Crystal Semiconductor CS4231
	graphics	Western Digital WD90C24A2, 1MB DRAM
	display	10.4-inch TFT color LCD, 640x480
		10.4-inch TFT color LCD, 800x600
Connectivity	serial / parallel	1 x 9-pin / 1 x enhanced parallel
	network	none
Expansion buses		PCMCIA: 2 x Type I or II, or 1 x Type III
Physical	dimensions	297 x 260 x 61 mm - 11.7 x 10.24 x 2.4 inches
	weight	3.2 kg (6.96 lbs) with battery
		3.6 kg (7.96 lbs) with battery and CD-ROM
		3.8 kg (8.28 lbs) with battery, CD-ROM, video camera

6.3 Advanced Function Support

These applications provided with the appropriate operating systems[1] , plus floating point
performance of the PowerPC processor, provide advanced function without additional
hardware:

---

[1]

Not all operating systems support all functions. Support for applications will only be provided on those
systems sold by IBM with operating systems included.

- IBM SOftMPEG Decoder for viewing MPEG 1 video/audio files
- IBM Video CD Player for viewing video CD-format movies
- IBM Soft MIDI Synthesizer for playing back high quality music
- Speech recognition, dictation and command navigation utilizing IBM VoiceType technology

6.3.1 Additional Information on MPEG and Music Synthesis

- IBM Video CD Player

    - The IBM Video CD Player provides the capability to view industry-standard MPEG digital video with every Power Personal Series system with the appropriate operating system support. It uses the IBM SoftMPEG Decoder to allow users to view movies distributed in Video-CD format. Video-CD is a format developed by Philips, JVC, MATSUSHITA, AND SONY. In addition, the IBM SoftMPEG Decoder supports the playback of MPEG 1 video clips.

        MPEG is an international standard for compressing and decompressing digital video and audio. The standard was developed by the Moving Pictures Experts Group (a joint ISO-IEC committee). MPEG is a popular video and audio distribution format because it achieves very favorable compression while enabling efficient decompression and high quality during playback. In the traditional PC market, special add-in boards are required to view MPEG files. IBM has developed software decompression algorithms capable of playing MPEG 1 using the advanced architecture and floating point capability of the PowerPC processors. With MPEG viewing capability on every desktop, the prospect of distributing information content in compressed audio and video form is enriched. The per seat cost for viewing such information is substantially reduced.

- SoftMIDI Synthesizer
    - IBM SoftMIDI Synthesizer uses high-quality audio sampling and supports the general MIDI standard. MIDI files allow complex musical compositions to be represented in a very compact form and played back on music synthesizers. This exciting music synthesizer is capable of responding to general MIDI files to produce high-quality music. The General MIDI files provide music for multimedia presentations, games, educational software and any other multimedia application with files much smaller than digitized .WAV files. It can be configured for different environments, providing entry level to high-level music sound quality without additional audio hardware. It supports up to 32 voices. Normally a special add-on card is required to provide wavetable music synthesis. The IBM SoftMIDI Synthesizer is another example of using the advanced architecture and floating point capability of the PowerPC processors.

Appendix A. What Is Multiprocessing?

This appendix is provided as an overview for readers who are not familiar with multiprocessing concepts.

Uni-processor designs have built-in bottlenecks. The address and data bus restrict data transfers to a one-at-a-time trickle of traffic. The program counter forces instructions to be executed in strict sequence. In the past, improvements in computer performance have been achieved simply by designing better, faster uni-processor machines. It now appears that further significant performance gains will need a different design.

Multiprocessing involves using more than one CPU. Multiprocessing can be categorized in a number of ways, but some of the more important aspects to consider are:

1. Do the processors share resources, or do they each have their own? Resources to consider include the operating system, memory, I/O channels, control units, files and drivers.

2. How are the processors connected? They might be in a single machine sharing a single bus or connected by other topologies (crossbar, grid, ring) or they might be in several machines using message-passing across a network.

3. Will all the processors be equal, or will some of them be specialized? For instance, all the processors can do integer arithmetic, but only one of them can do floating point.

4. Will parallel programming be supported? The act of sharing the parts of a program (breaking the code up, copying relevant data to each of the parts, finding an idle processor, collecting the results and synchronizing any inter-process interactions) represents an extra task in itself.

5. Will it be easy to enhance/upgrade the system at a later date? Usually the addition of a new processor will not cause system throughput to increase by the rated capacity of the new processor, because there is

   • Additional operating system overhead

   • Increased contention for system resources

   • Hardware delays in switching and routing transmissions between an increased number of components.

6. What happens if one of the processors fails? One of the most important capabilities of the multiprocessor operating systems is their ability to withstand equipment failures in individual processors and to continue operation.

Loosely coupled multiprocessing involves connecting two or more independent computer systems via a communication link. Each system has its own operating system and storage. The systems can function independently and can communicate when necessary. The separate systems can access each other's files across the communications link, and in some cases, they can switch tasks to more lightly loaded processors to achieve a degree of load balancing.

Tightly coupled multiprocessing uses a single storage shared by the various processors and a single operating system that controls all the processors and system hardware.

There are three basic operating system organizations for multiprocessors:

1. Master/slave model

   One processor is designated as the master and the others are the slaves. The master is general-purpose processor and performs I/O as well as computation. The slave processors perform only computation. The processors are considered asymmetric (not equivalent) since only the master can do I/O as well as computation. Utilization of a slave may be poor if the master does not service slave requests efficiently enough. I/O-bound jobs may not run efficiently since only the master does I/O. Failure of the master is catastrophic.

2. Separate execution model

   Each processor has its own operating system and responds to interrupts from users running on that processor. A process assigned to run on a particular processor runs to completion. It is possible for some of the processors to remain idle while one processor executes a lengthy process. Some tables are global to the entire system and access to these tables must be carefully controlled. Each processor controls its own dedicated resources, such as files and I/O devices.

3. Symmetric multiprocessing model

   All of the processors are functionally equivalent and can perform I/O and computation. The operating system manages a pool of identical processors, any one of which may be used to control any I/O devices or reference any storage unit. Conflicts between processors attempting to access the same storage at the same time are ordinarily resolved by hardware. Multiple tables in the kernel can be accessed by different processes simultaneously. Conflicts in access to system-wide tables are ordinarily resolved by software. A process may be run at different times by any of the processors and at any given time, several processors may execute operating system functions in kernel mode.

A two-processor system (for example) can do more work than a uni-processor system, but it will not do twice as much as a uni-processor system. This is because there is some overhead associated with adding CPUs. The major impediments to the scalability of MP machines are:

1. Contention for the operating system

   An MP can have multiple processes accessing kernel data structures simultaneously. Therefore, mutual exclusion locks must be placed around many of these structures (or the code accessing them) to guarantee atomizing. These locks degrade performance by:

   - Increasing the path length of the system calls.

   - Causing collisions when multiple processes try to access a protected area simultaneously. In this case, all but one process will have to wait for the critical data structure to become free.

2. Contention for the system bus

3. Increased overhead of cache misses due to the coherency protocol

   A cache miss is more costly on a multiprocessor system than it is on a uni-processor system. This is because if data is marked *dirty* in the cache of another processor, the *dirty* data must be written to memory before it can be accessed and used on another processor.

4. Contention and communication within the application

   Multiple tasks within an application may be executing on different processors. If at some point, they need to synchronize, the application overhead is increased by communication between the tasks and waiting for each task to get to the synchronization point.

Appendix B. The PowerPC Instruction Set

This appendix provides information on the relationship between the instruction sets used for the POWER, POWER2, PowerPC Architecture and the PowerPC 601 microprocessor. Figure B-1 on page B-2 shows the relationship between the instruction sets.

The PowerPC 601 processor was intended to be bridge processor from POWER to PowerPC. The PowerPC 601, in fact, implements nearly all of both, POWER and 32-bit PowerPC instruction sets. POWER2 added several new instructions to extend POWER for technical applications, namely load/store, floating-point quad, floating square root, and floating-point to integer convert. POWER2 applications which exploit these instructions will fail on a POWER machine. While square root and integer convert are not necessarily at issue, being confined mostly to math libraries (enabling applications to run well on both POWER and POWER2), the load/store quad instructions are another matter. These instructions would tend to get used in mainline code and the performance ramifications do not make them good candidates for emulation. An application choosing to exploit these also explicitly chooses to discard POWER compatibility.

The PowerPC instruction set can be characterized as being based on the POWER instruction set with less a number of instructions. PowerPC also proceed to add a number of new instruction, some common with POWER2, as well as others not either POWER or POWER2. The POWER instructions discarded by PowerPC were targeted for emulation as their frequency of use was projected to be minimal.

There is a set of instructions common to each of the architectures that compilers will restrict themselves to when requested which will allow the program to execute on any of the three architectures with minimal emulation activity. However, program binaries which employ POWER2's load/store quad ops will not execute on either POWER or PowerPC Program binaries which exploit PowerPC-unique ops will either run less than optimal, if at all on POWER and POWER2. POWER specific program binaries should run well on POWER2 and statistics indicate should run reasonable well on PowerPC as well with some amount of emulation.

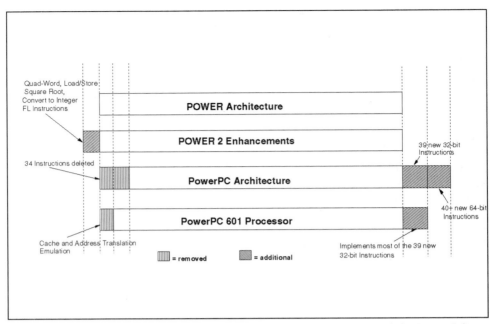

Figure B-1. *Relationship between POWER, POWER2, PowerPC and the PowerPC 601 Instruction Set*

Table B-1 provides a list of of the 32-bit and 64-bit PowerPC instructions.

Table B-1 (Page 1 of 7). The PowerPC Instruction Set			
Mnemonic	**32-bit**	**64-bit**	**Description**
addx	√	√	*add*
addcx	√	√	*add carrying*
addex	√	√	*add extended*
addi	√	√	*add immediate*
addic	√	√	*add immediate carrying*
addic.	√	√	*add immediate carrying and record*
addis	√	√	*add immediate shifted*
addmex	√	√	*add to minus one extended*
addzex	√	√	*add to zero extended*
andx	√	√	*and*
andcx	√	√	*and with complement*
andi.	√	√	*and immediate*
andis	√	√	*and immediate shifted*
bx	√	√	*branch*
bcx	√	√	*branch conditional*
bcctrx	√	√	*branch conditional to count register*

Mnemonic	32-bit	64-bit	Description
bclrx	√	√	*branch conditional to link register*
cmp	√	√	*compare*
cmpi	√	√	*compare immediate*
cmpl	√	√	*compare logical*
cmpli	√	√	*compare logical immediate*
cntlzdx	√	√	*count leading zeros doubleword*
cntlzwx	√	√	*count leading zeros word*
crand	√	√	*condition register and*
crandc	√	√	*condition register and with complement*
creqv	√	√	*condition register equivalent*
crnand	√	√	*condition register nand*
crnor	√	√	*condition register nor*
cror	√	√	*condition register or*
crorc	√	√	*condition register or with complement*
crxor	√	√	*condition register xor*
dcbf	√	√	*data cache block flush*
dcbi	√	√	*data cache block invalidate*
dcbst	√	√	*data cache block store*
dcbt	√	√	*data cache block touch*
dcbtst	√	√	*data cache block touch for store*
dcbz	√	√	*data cache block set to zero*
divdx		√	*divide doubleword*
divdux		√	*divide doubleword unsigned*
divwx	√	√	*divide word*
divwux	√	√	*divide word unsigned*
eciwx	√	√	*external control in word indexed*
ecowx	√	√	*external control out word indexed*
eieio	√	√	*enforce in-order execution of I/O*
eqvx		√	*equivalent*
extsbx	√	√	*extend sign bite*
extshx	√	√	*extend sign halfword*
extswx		√	*extend sign word*
fabsx	√	√	*floating absolute value*
faddx	√	√	*floating add*
faddsx	√	√	*floating add single*
fcfidx		√	*floating convert from integer doubleword*
fcmpo	√	√	*floating compare ordered*
fcmpu	√	√	*floating compare unordered*
fctidx		√	*floating convert to integer doubleword*
fctidzx		√	*floating convert to integer doubleword with round toward zero*
fctiwx	√	√	*floating convert to integer word*

Mnemonic	32-bit	64-bit	Description
fctiwzx	√	√	*floating convert to integer word with round toward zero*
fdiv	√	√	*floating divide*
fdivsx	√	√	*floating divide single*
fmaddx	√	√	*floating multiple-add*
fmaddsx	√	√	*floating multiple-add single*
fmrx	√	√	*floating move register*
fmsubx	√	√	*floating multiply-subtract*
fmsubsx	√	√	*floating multiply-subtract single*
fmulx	√	√	*floating multiply*
fmulsx	√	√	*floating multiply single*
fnabsx	√	√	*floating negative absolute value*
fnegx	√	√	*floating negate*
fnmaddx	√	√	*floating negative multiply-add*
fnmaddsx	√	√	*floating negative multiply-add single*
fnmsubx	√	√	*floating negative multiply-subtract*
fnmsubsx	√	√	*floating negative multiply-subtract single*
fresx	√	√	*floating reciprocal estimate single*
frspx	√	√	*floating round to single-precision*
frsqrtex	√	√	*floating reciprocal square root estimate*
fselx	√	√	*floating select*
fsqrtx	√	√	*floating square root*
fsqrtsx	√	√	*floating square root single*
fsubx	√	√	*floating subtract*
fsubsx	√	√	*floating subtract single*
icbi	√	√	*instruction cache block invalidate*
isync	√	√	*instruction synchronize*
lbz	√	√	*load byte and zero*
lbzu	√	√	*load byte and zero with update*
lbzux	√	√	*load byte and zero with update indexed*
lbzx	√	√	*load byte and zero indexed*
ld		√	*load doubleword*
ldarx		√	*load doubleword and reserve index*
ldu		√	*load doubleword with update*
ldux		√	*load doubleword with update indexed*
ldx		√	*load doubleword indexed*
lfd	√	√	*load floating-point double*
lfdu	√	√	*load floating-point double with update*
lfdux	√	√	*load floating-point double with update indexed*
lfdx	√	√	*load floating-point double indexed*
lfs	√	√	*load floating-point single*

Mnemonic	32-bit	64-bit	Description
lfsu	√	√	*load floating-point single with update*
lfsux	√	√	*load floating-point single with update indexed*
lfsx	√	√	*load floating-point single indexed*
lha	√	√	*load halfword algebraic*
lhau	√	√	*load halfword algebraic with update*
lhaux	√	√	*load halfword algebraic with update indexed*
lhax	√	√	*load halfword algebraic indexed*
lhbrx	√	√	*load halfword byte-reserved indexed*
lhz	√	√	*load halfwaord and zero*
lhzu	√	√	*load halfword and zero with update*
lhzux	√	√	*load halfword and zero with update indexed*
lhzx	√	√	*load halfword and zero indexed*
lmw	√	√	*load multiple word*
lswi	√	√	*load string word immediate*
lswx	√	√	*load string word indexed*
lwa		√	*load word algebraic*
lwarx	√	√	*load word and reserve indexed*
lwaux		√	*load word algebraic with update indexed*
lwax		√	*load word algebraic indexed*
lwbrx	√	√	*load word byte-reserve indexed*
lwz	√	√	*load word and zero*
lwzu	√	√	*load word and zero with update*
lwzux	√	√	*load word and zero with update indexed*
lwzx	√	√	*load word and zero indexed*
mcrf	√	√	*move condition field register*
mcrfs	√	√	*move condition field register rom FPSCR*
mcrxr	√	√	*move to condition register rom XER*
mcfr	√	√	*move from condition register*
mffsx	√	√	*move from FPSCR*
mfmsr	√	√	*move from machine state register*
mfspr	√	√	*move from special purpose register*
mfsr	√		*move from segment register*
mfsrin	√		*move from segment register indirect*
mftb	√	√	*move from time base*
mtcrf	√	√	*move to condition register field*
mtfsb0x	√	√	*move to FPSCR bit 0*
mtfsb1x	√	√	*move to FPSCR bit 1*
mtffsx	√	√	*move to FPSCR fields*
mtfsifx	√	√	*move to FPSCR fields immediate*

Mnemonic	32-bit	64-bit	Description
mtmsr	√	√	*move to machine state register*
mtsr	√		*move to segment register*
mtsrin	√		*move to segment register indirect*
mulhdx		√	*multiply high doubleword*
mulhdux		√	*multiply high doubleword unsigned*
mulhwx	√	√	*multiply high word*
mulhwux	√	√	*multiply high word unsigned*
mulldx	√	√	*multiply low doubleword*
mulli	√	√	*multiply low immediate*
mullwx	√	√	*multiply low word*
nandx	√	√	*nand*
negx	√	√	*negate*
norx	√	√	*nor*
orx	√	√	*or*
orcx	√	√	*or with complement*
ori	√	√	*or immediate*
oris	√	√	*or immediate shifted*
rfi	√	√	*return rom interrupt*
rldclx		√	*rotate left doubleword then clear left*
rldcrx		√	*rotate left doubleword then clear right*
rldicx		√	*rotate left doubleword immediate then clear*
rldiclx		√	*rotate left doubleword immediate then clear left*
rldicrx		√	*rotate left doubleword immediate then clear right*
rldimix		√	*rotate left doubleword immediate then mask insert*
rlwimix	√	√	*rotate left word immediate then mask insert*
rlwinmx	√	√	*rotate left word immediate then and with mask*
rlwnmx	√	√	*rotate left word then and with mask*
sc	√	√	*system call*
slbia		√	*slb invalidate call*
slbie		√	*slb invalidate entry*
sldx		√	*shift left double word*
slwx	√	√	*shift left word*
sradx		√	*shift algebraic doubleword*
sradix		√	*shift right algebraic doubleword immediate*
srawx	√	√	*shift right algebraic word*
srawix	√	√	*shift right algebraic word immediate*
srdx		√	*shift right doubleword*
srwx	√	√	*floating negative multiply-add*

Mnemonic	32-bit	64-bit	Description
stb	√	√	*store byte*
stbu	√	√	*store byte with update*
stbux	√	√	*store byte with update indexed*
stbx	√	√	*store byte indexed*
std		√	*store doubleword*
stdcx		√	*store doubleword conditional indexed*
stdu		√	*store doubleword with update*
stdux		√	*store doubleword indexed with update*
stdx		√	*store doubleword indexed*
stfd	√	√	*store floating-point double*
stfdu	√	√	*store floating-point double with update*
stfdux	√	√	*store floating-point double with update indexed*
stfdx	√	√	*store floating-point double indexed*
stiwx	√	√	*store floating-point as integer word indexed*
stfs	√	√	*store floating-point single*
stfsu	√	√	*store floating-point single with update*
stfsux	√	√	*store floating-point single with update indexed*
stfsx	√	√	*store floating-point single indexed*
sth	√	√	*store halfword*
sthbrx	√	√	*store halfword byte-reserved indexed*
sthu	√	√	*store halfword with update*
sthux	√	√	*store halfword with update indexed*
sthx	√	√	*store halfword indexed*
stmw	√	√	*store multiple word*
stswi	√	√	*store string word immediate*
stswx	√	√	*store string word indexed*
stw	√	√	*store word*
stwbrx	√	√	*store word byte-reverse indexed*
stwcx	√	√	*store word conditional indexed*
stwu	√	√	*store word with update*
stwux	√	√	*store word with update indexed*
stwx	√	√	*store word indexed*
subfx	√	√	*substract from*
subfcx	√	√	*substract from carrying*
subfex	√	√	*substract from immediate carrying*
subfmex	√	√	*substract from minus one extended*
subfzex	√	√	*substract from zero extended*
sync	√	√	*synchronize*

Table B-2 on page B-8 provides a list of PowerPC instructions not supported by the PowerPC 601 processor.

Table B-2. *PowerPC Instructions not Supported by the PowerPC 601 Processor*

Mnemonic	Description
fresx	*floating-point reciprocal estimate single precision*
frsqrtex	*floating-point reciprocal square root estimate*
fselx	*floating-point select*
fsqrtx	*floating-point square root*
fsqrtsx	*floating-point square root single precision*
mftb	*move from time base*
stfiwx	*store floating-point as integer word indexed*
tlbia	*translation lookaside buffer invalidate all*
tlbsync	*translation lookaside buffer synchronize*

Table B-3 provides a list of POWER instructions deleted from the PowerPC Architecture. However, some of the instructions are used by the PowerPC 601 processor, as the PowerPC 601 processor is a "bridge" processor between the POWER and PowerPC technology.

Table B-3 (Page 1 of 2). *Power Instructions Deleted from the PowerPC Architecture*

Mnemonic	Description	601
absx	*absolute*	Yes
clcs	*cache line compute size*	Yes
clf	*cach line flash*	No
cli	*cache line invalidate*	No
dclst	*data cache line store*	No
divx	*divide*	Yes
divsx	*divide short*	Yes
dozx	*difference or zero*	Yes
dozi	*difference or zero immediate*	Yes
lscbxx	*load string and compare byte indexed*	Yes
maskgx	*mask generate*	Yes
maskirx	*mask insert from register*	Yes
mfsri	*move from segment register indirect*	No
mulx	*multiply*	Yes
nabsx	*negative absolute*	Yes
rac	*real address compute*	No
rlmix	*rotate left then mask insert*	Yes
rribx	*rotate right and insert bit*	Yes
slex	*shift left extended*	Yes
sleqx	*shift left extended with MQ*	Yes

Table B-3 (Page 2 of 2). *Power Instructions Deleted from the PowerPC Architecture*

Mnemonic	Description	601
sliqx	*shift left immediate with MQ*	Yes
sllqx	*shift left long with MQ*	Yes
slqx	*shift left with MQ*	Yes
sraiqx	*shift right algebraic immediate with MQ*	Yes
sraqx	*shift right algebraic with MQ*	Yes
srex	*shift right extended*	Yes
sreax	*shift right extended algebraic*	Yes
sreqx	*shift right extended with MQ*	Yes
sriqx	*shift right immediate with MQ*	Yes
srlqx	*shift right long with MQ*	Yes
srqx	*shift right with MQ*	Yes

Glossary

A

Abstraction Software Layer. Separates the hardware from the software.

Application Binary Interface. Enables applications to run on all available PowerOpen-compliant operating systems no matter which PowerPC based hardware it runs on.

Application Binary Interface (ABI). An ABI is a set of guidelines describing how binary code should be structured so that applications and code will run unchanged across systems from multiple vendors. The ABI is a more specific machine-level API.

Application Programming Interface. A library of routines for application programmers.

Asymmetric Multiprocessing. See Multiprocessing.

Asynchronous Exceptions. Exceptions that are caused by external events or other conditions not connected to whatever the CPU is processing at the time that the exception occurred. Contrast with Synchronous Exceptions.

B

Bi-Endian Support. Support in the processor architecture for both Big-Endian and Little-Endian byte ordering.

Big-Endian Byte Ordering. A method of storing and accessing multi-byte data types. The data is stored starting with the most significant byte and ending with the least significant.

Block. In the PowerPC Architecture, a special memory partition which can be 128KB to 256MB in size. It is specially defined to allow for quick access.

Block Address Translation. The process of translating the logical address of a block into the physical address.

Block Address Translation Registers. The registers that store the locations of blocks in memory. Used in the block address translation process.

Boot Time Abstraction Layer. Collection of firmware and software which abstracts the hardware at boot time.

Branch Look-Ahead. The technique of inspecting the instruction queue to detect branch instructions in the instruction stream. The aim is to execute branch instructions early enough to achieve zero-cycle branching.

C

Cache. A high-speed storage buffer that contains frequently accessed instructions and data; it is used to reduce access time.

Cache Coherency. The situation where multiple cache units sharing one main memory space have an accurate view of the contents of memory.

Cooperative Multitasking. A form of multitasking in which a thread (or application) decides when to stop executing in order to let other threads run.

CD-ROM. Compact disk-read only memory. A disc that you can only read data from. Data cannot be written to a CD-ROM.

Coprocessor. A microprocessor on an expansion board or planar that extends the address range of the main processor or adds specialized instructions to handle a particular category of operations.

Critical Word First. A cache data transfer policy. When the CPU needs a piece of data that is not in cache, the loading from memory always occurs with the piece of data that the CPU needs first, regardless of its place in the cache block.

Cycles per Instruction. The average number of clock cycles needed to complete executing one instruction.

Cycle Time. The amount of time taken to complete one CPU cycle.

D

Device. An input/output (I/O) unit such as a terminal, a display, or a printer.

Device Driver. A file that contains the code needed to attach and use a device.

Direct Access Storage Device (DASD). A device in which access time is effectively independent of the location of the data.

Direct Address Translation. The process of using a logical address as the physical address in a memory access. Used when address translation is disabled.

DMA. Direct memory access; technique by which transfers to and from system memory are made by an independent control chip rather than by the system's main processor, thereby resulting in improved overall performance.

DOS. Disk operating system. A program that controls the operation of an IBM Personal Computer, PS/1, PS/2, or PS/ValuePoint and the execution of application programs.

Dynamic Power Management Mode. A mechanism in the PowerPC 603 chip to minimize power consumption during normal operation of the CPU. It does this by detecting any functional unit that is idle and putting this unit in a low-power state.

E

Error Checking and Correction (ECC). In a processing unit, the detection and correction of all single-bit errors, plus the detection of double-bit and some multiple-bit errors.

EPROM. Erasable programmable read-only memory. Programmable read-only memory that is read-only in normal use but can be erased by a special technique and then reprogrammed.

EMS. Expanded memory specification; term used to describe the standard developed by Lotus, Intel and Microsoft for access to expanded memory by real mode DOS application.

Exception. An abnormal or error condition during processing. May be caused by a variety of fatal or non-fatal events. See asynchronous exceptions, synchronous exceptions, precise exceptions and imprecise exceptions.

Extended I/O Controller. This controller control a host of functions including the NVRAM, real-time clock, LED indicators and UMCU

F

FAT. File allocation table; term used to describe the file system implemented by DOS. This file system uses a file allocation table to contain the physical sector addresses of all files on the disk.

First In/First Out (FIFO). A queuing technique in which the next item to be retrieved is the item that has been in the queue for the longest time.

Fixed Disk. A flat, circular, nonremovable plate with a surface layer on which data can be stored by magnetic recording.

FLASH. An electrically erasable programmable read only memory (EEPROM) module that can be updated by diskette

H

Hardware Architecture. Hardware architecture is the logical structure and functional characteristics of a computer including the relationships among its hardware and software.

I

I/O Controller Interface Access. A method of accessing I/O devices from programs. It uses message passing between the CPU and the I/O controller to communicate.

I/O Controller Interface Translation. The process of using a logical address to generate the I/O controller address and the messages used to communicate with an I/O controller. This is the address translation process used for I/O controller interface accesses.

I/O Memory. I/O memory is the area in memory that refers to the addresses where I/O devices reside

Imprecise Exceptions. Exceptions that are usually caused by a very serious failure or non-recoverable condition. They may cause the CPU to halt processing or stop execution of some program. Contrast with precise exceptions.

Intelligent Agent. A part in an application that uses artificial intelligence to enable the computer to understand natural language commands, and responding with complex series of tasks based upon those commands.

Interprocess Communication (IPC). The basic mechanism by which threads running in different tasks can communicate with each other.

Initial Program Load (IPL). (1) The initialization procedure that starts an operating system. (2) The process of loading programs and preparing a system to run jobs.

Interface. A shared boundary between two or more entities. An interface may be a hardware component to link two devices or a portion of storage or registers accessed by two or more computer programs.

International Organization for Standardization (ISO). An organization of national standards bodies from various countries established to promote the development of standards to facilitate international exchange of goods and services, and develop cooperation in intellectual, scientific, technological and economic activity.

Interrupt. A suspension of a process, such as execution of a computer program caused by an external event, and performed in such a way that the process can be resumed.

K

Kernel Programming Interface. Provides the interface to kernel process and device drivers.

Kilobyte (KB). 1024 bytes for processor and data storage (memory) size; otherwise, 1000 bytes.

L

Little-Endian Byte Ordering. A method of storing and accessing multi-byte data types. The data is stored starting with the least significant byte and ending with the most significant.

Liquid Crystal Display (LCD). A display device that creates characters by means of reflected light on patterns formed by a liquid that becomes opaque when it is energized.

Load/Store Architecture. The method of moving data between CPU registers and main memory using specialized load and store instructions and using only register operands in computational instructions.

M

Machine Abstractions. see abstraction software layer

Math Coprocessor. In a personal computer, a microprocessor on an expansion board that supplements the operations of the processor in the system unit, enabling a personal computer to perform complex mathematical operations in parallel with other operations.

Megabyte (MB). 1,048,576 bytes.

MEI Protocol. A simplified version of the MESI protocol (see MESI Protocol). Does not have a shared state.

MESI Protocol. A mechanism to keep track of the state of data in a cache unit. Cache lines can be marked as being in a modified, exclusive, invalid or shared state.

Multiprocessing. Multiprocessing is the ability to execute threads on more than one processor concurrently. In symmetric multiprocessing, the operating system as well as other processes can have threads executing on multiple processors (as opposed to asymmetric multiprocessing, in which the operating system executes only one processor).

N

Native I/O Controller. The native I/O controller is a controller chip that controls the diskette drive, serial port, parallel port and integrated IDE.

O

Operating Environment Architecture. A layer of the PowerPC Architecture that defines the memory management and exception models.

Operating System. The software that controls the running of programs. An operating system may provide services such as resource allocation, scheduling, input/output (I/O) control and data management.

Out-of-Order Execution. The situation in a superscalar CPU where instructions are allowed to execute without following the order in which they are coded in the program.

P

Page. A 4MB partition of a segment. (See Segment)

Path Length. The number of computer instructions needed to perform a task.

Performance Optimization With Enhanced RISC (POWER). IBM's second-generation RISC architecture. Serves as the underlying processor architecture for IBM's RISC System/6000 family of products.

PCI bridge and memory controller. This controlle consists of two modules that makes a connection between the memory, processor and PCI bus

PCI-ISA bridge controller. A bridge between to the ISA bus is provide by this controller.

Pipelining. A technique where processing of an instruction is divided into several stages and multiple instructions are processed concurrently, with each instruction in different stages of processing (assembly-line style).

Planar. Also known as the motherboard. The largest electronic board in a computer which connects the various subsystems together.

Power-on Self Test (POST). A series of diagnostic tests that are run automatically each time the computer's power is turned on.

PowerOpen Association. Membership driven organization chartered to manage the evolution of the PowerOpen application binary interface (ABI).

PowerOpen. A company formed by IBM and Apple dedicated to promoting the PowerOpen environment. The PowerOpen environment defines a standard UNIX platform that allows developers to write UNIX-based software that can be ported to any PowerOpen-compliant operating system

PowerPC Reference Platform Specification. A document created by IBM and widely distributed to vendors who wish to offer PowerPC hardware and software. It defines a suggested hardware configuration for PowerPC machines.

Precise Exceptions. Exceptions where the exact cause is known and the machine state at the time of exception is known. Contrast with imprecise exceptions.

Preemptive Multitasking. A form of multitasking in which the operating system periodically interrupts the execution of a thread in order to let other threads execute. This prevents monopolization of the processor by one thread.

Principle of Locality. The probability that if the CPU fetches a piece of program code from memory, the next piece that it needs is next to or near to the one currently being fetched.

Process. An address space and collection of threads. This can be thought of as an abstraction of a running program. It typically contains the executable, the program's data, the stack, program counter, stack pointer, and other registers. Essentially this is all of the information needed to run the program. A process is created, managed, and terminated by the operating system. A process is also sometimes refered to as a task, and consists of executable entities called threads. A process can become a parent process by creating other (child) processes which may inherit some or all of the parent process's resources.

R

Random Access Memory (RAM). A computer's or adapter's volatile storage area into which data may be entered or retrieved from in a non-sequential manner.

Reduced Instruction Set Cycles. A processor architecture designed to produce the optimal value of Path Length x Cycles per Instruction.

Run Time Abstraction Layer. Collection of data and software that abstracts hardware from the operating system kernel. The run time abstraction layer is made of system abstraction software and device drivers.

S

Segment. A 256MB partition of the PowerPC logical address space.

Snooping. A technique to maintain cache coherency (see cache coherency). All cache units watch the system bus. When a cache unit accesses main memory, all the other cache devices know about the access and can take action to ensure that they maintain a coherent view of memory.

Static Branch Prediction. A scheme that attempts to predict in a conditional branch instruction, whether or not the branch will occur. The prediction that the scheme gives is fixed and does not change with the circumstances.

Subsystem. A secondary or subordinate system, or programming support, usually capable of operating independently of asychronously with a controlling system.

Superscalar Design. The concept of dispatching and executing multiple instructions in parallel using multiple execution units within a CPU.

Supervisor-Level Programs. Programs that have the authority to perform privileged operations. These privileged operations usually involve using or changing some protected critical system resources. Contrast with User-level Programs.

Symmetric Multiprocessing. See Multiprocessing.

Synchronous Exceptions. Exceptions that are caused by the instructions that the CPU is processing at a particular moment. Contrast with asynchronous exceptions.

System I/O. The system I/O is the area in the memory map that handles the addressing and communication for all I/O functions

System Memory. The portion of memory where executable instructions reside is called the system memory

System ROM. The system ROM is the are in memory where power-on firmware and boot firmware are stored. It is normally implemented as ROM, EPROM, EEPROM or FLASH ROM.

T

Translation Lookaside Buffer. Fast hardware buffer that contains the most recent logical to physical address mappings.

Thread. The entities which actually execute in a process's address space.

U

UMCU. The universal micro control unit manages basic power functions. It is alive even when power is switched off.

User Instruction Set Architecture. A layer of the PowerPC Architecture that defines the user-level programming environment and the programming model for a uniprocessor environment.

User-Level Programs. Programs that execute with normal privileges. These programs do not have the authority to manipulate protected system resources. Contrast with supervisor-level programs.

V

Virtual 8086 Mode. Mode of operation of the Intel 32-bit processors, which allows the processor to execute multiple concurrent tasks with each regarding the processor as its own distinct 8086 processor. This mode of operation provides multitasking and memory protection between the virtual 8086 tasks. Also known as V86 mode.

Virtual Environment Architecture. A layer of the PowerPC Architecture that defines the programming model for a multiprocessing environment.

W

WIM Bits. Three bits that define the caching attributes of a page or block.

Write Back. A policy that can be implemented to control the behavior of the cache system. The write back policy states that any modified data need not be reflected in memory immediately. It must be copied out when the cache unit detects that another cache device wants to access the same piece of data in memory.

Write Through. A policy that can be implemented to control the behavior of the cache system. The write through policy states that any cache data that is modified must be copied out to main memory immediately.

Z

Zero-Cycle Branching. The ability to detect and resolve branch instructions early enough to ensure an uninterrupted instruction stream and avoid branch delay.

List of Abbreviations

ABI	Application Binary Interface	*CR*	Condition Register
AIX	Advanced Interactive eXecutive	*CU*	Completion Unit
		DAC	Digital to Analog Converter
ANSI	American National Standards Institute	*DASD*	Direct Access Storage Device
		DDK	Device Driver Development Kit
AT	Advanced Technology	*DIMM*	Dual In-Line Memory Module
ATM	Asynchronous Transfer Mode	*DMA*	Direct Memory Access
BAT	Block Address Translation	*D-MMU*	Data Memory Management Unit
BIOS	Basic Input/Output System	*DOS*	Disk Operating System
BP	Branch Processor	*DPMI*	DOS Protected Mode Interface
BTAS	Boot Time Abstraction Layer	*DRAM*	Dynamic Random Access Memory
CD	Compact Disk	*DSOM*	Distributed System Object Model
CD-ROM	Compact Disk - Read Only Memory		
CISC	Complex Instruction Set Computer	*DSP*	Digital Signal Processor
		ECC	Error Checking and Correcting
CMOS	Complementary Metal Oxide Semiconductor	*ECP*	Extended Capabilities Port
CODEC	Coder Decoder	*EEPROM*	Electrically Erasable Programmable Read Only Memory
CORBA	Common Object Request Broker Architecture		
CPU	Central Processing Unit		

EIA	Electronics Industries Association (USA)	**GUI**	Graphic User Interface
EISA	Extended Industry Standard Architecture	**HDD**	Hard Disk Drive
		HPFS	High Performance File System
ELF	Executable and Linking Format	**Hz**	Hertz
EMS	Expanded Memory Specification	**IBM**	International Business Machines Corporation
EPA	Environmental Protection Agency (USA, government)	**IC**	Integrated Circuit
		ICU	Instruction Cache Unit
EPROM	Erasable Programmable Read Only Memory	**IDE**	Integrated Device Electronics
		IDE	Integrated Development Environment
ESDI	Enhanced Small Device Interface	**IEEE**	Institute of Electrical and Electronics Engineers
FAT	File Alocation Table		
FAX	Facsimile	**I/O**	Input/Output
FDD	Floppy Disk Drive	**IML**	Initial Microcode Load
FIFO	First In/First Out	**I-MMU**	Instruction Memory Management Unit
FP	Floating-Point		
FPR	Floating-Point Register	**IPL**	Initial Program Load
FPSCR	Floating-Point Status and Control Register	**IRQ**	Interrupt Request
		ISA	Industry Standard Architecture
FPU	Floating-Point Unit	**ISO**	International Organization for Standardization
FXU	Fixed-Point Unit		
GB	Gigabyte	**IST**	Instruction Set Translator
GPR	General-Purpose Register		

ITSO	International Technical Support Organization	*MHz*	Mega Hertz
		MIDI	Musical Instrument Digital Interface
IU	Instruction Unit		
JEDEC	Joint Electron Device Engineering Council	*MMU*	Memory Management Unit
		MSR	Machine State Register
JEIDA	Japan Electronic Industry Development Association	*MVM*	Multiple Virtual Machine
		NiCad	Nickel-Cadmium
KB	Kilobyte	*NiCd*	Nickel-Cadmium
KBI	Kernel Binary Interface	*NiMH*	Nickel Metal Hydride
kHz	Kilohertz	*NTSC*	National Television Standards Committee (USA)
LAN	Local Area Network		
LCD	Liquid Crystal Display	*NVRAM*	Non-Volatile Random Access Memory
LED	Light Emitting Diode		
		OEA	Operating Environment Architecture
LIM	Lotus Intel Microsoft		
LSU	Load/Store Unit	*OEM*	Original Equipment Manufacturer
MAS	Macintosh Application Services		
		OS	Operating System
MB	Megabyte	*OSF*	Open Software Foundation
MCA	Micro Channel Architecture		
		OS/2	Operating System/2
MEI	Modified, Exclusive, Invalid	*PC*	Personal Computer
MESI	Modified, Exclusive, Shared, Invalid	*PC-DOS*	Personal Computer Disk Operating System
MFM	Modified Frequency Modulation	*PCHE*	PC Hardware Environment

PCI	Peripheral Component Interconnect	**RGB**	Red Green Blue
PCMCIA	Personal Computer Memory Card International Association	**RISC**	Reduced Instruction Set Computer
		ROM	Read Only Memory
POE	PowerOpen Environment	**RS/6000**	RISC System/6000
POSIX	Portable Operating System Interface for Computer Environment	**RTAS**	Run Time Abstraction Layer Software
		RTC	Real-Time Clock
		SCB	Subsystem Control Block
POST	Power on Self Test	**SCSI**	Small Computer System Interface
POWER	Performance Optimized with Enhanced RISC	**SDK**	Software Development Kit
PowerPC	Performance Optimized with Enhanced RISC Performance Chip	**SIMM**	Single In-Line Memory Module
		SOHO	Small Office/Home Office
PowerPC SIL	The PowerPC System Information Library	**SMP**	Symmetric MultiProcessing
		SOM	System Object Model
PS/2	Personal System/2	**SPRs**	Special Purpose Registers
PSM	Platform-Specific Module	**SR**	Segment Register
PTE	Page Table Entry	**SRAM**	Static Random Access Memory
RAID	Redundant Array of Inexpensive Disks		
		SRU	System Register Unit
RAM	Random Access Memory	**STN**	Super Twisted Nematic (portable PC screen technology)
RAMDAC	Random Access Memory and Digital to Analog Converter		

SVGA	Super Video Graphics Array/Adapter	*VEA*	Virtual Environment Architecture
SVR4	Unix System V Release 4	*VESA*	Video Electronics Standards Association
TCP/IP	Transmmission Control Protocol/Internet Protocol	*VGA*	Video Graphics Array/Adapter
		VL-Bus	VESA Local Bus
TFT	Thin-Film Transistor	*VLSI*	Very Large Scale Integration
TIA	Telecommunications Industries Association (part of EIA)	*VPD*	Vital Product Data
		VRAM	Video RAM
TLB	Translation Lookaside Buffer	*XCOFF*	eXtended COFF (Common Object File Format)
UISA	User Instruction Set Architecture	*XMS*	eXtended Memory Specification
UMCU	Universal Micro Control Unit		

Index

Numerics

A

B

C